E N A C T M E N T S

Edited by Richard Schechner

To perform is to imagine, represent, live and enact present circumstances, past events and future possibilities. Performance takes place across a very broad range of venues from city streets to the countryside, in theatres and in offices, on battlefields and in hospital operating rooms. The genres of performance are many, from the arts to the myriad performances of everyday life, from courtrooms to legislative chambers, from theatres to wars to circuses.

ENACTMENTS will encompass performance in as many of its aspects and realities as there are authors able to write about them.

ENACTMENTS will include active scholarship, readable thought and engaged analysis across the broad spectrum of performance studies.

Rhythm Field

THE
DANCE
OF
MOLISSA
FENLEY

Edited by
Ann Murphy
and
Molissa Fenley

Seagull Books
LONDON NEW YORK CALCUTTA

A special thank you to Karma Pippin, archivist to the Molissa Fenley Archive housed within Special Collections at the Olin Library, Mills College, Oakland, California.

Molissa Fenley

SEAGULL BOOKS, 2015

ISBN 978 0 8574 2 219 4

British Library Cataloguing-in-Publication Data

A catalogue record for this book is available from the British Library

Book designed and typeset by Manasij Dutta, Seagull Books, Calcutta, India

Printed and bound by Hyam Enterprises, Calcutta, India

CONTENTS

(Clockwise from top left) IMAGE 1 *Hemispheres* (1983); Scottie Mirviss, Molissa Fenley, Silvia Martins in performance at the Brooklyn Academy of Music, New York. Photograph by Beatriz Schiller © 1984. IMAGE 2 *Hemispheres* (1983); Scottie Mirviss, Molissa Fenley, Silvia Martins in rehearsal at the Harkness Ballet Center, New York. Photograph by Peter Hujar © 1984. IMAGE 3 *Esperanto* (1985); Scottie Mirviss, Jill Diamond, Molissa Fenley, Elizabeth Benjamin (hidden) in performance at the Joyce Theater, New York; costumes by Jean-Paul Gaultier. Photograph by Helma Klooss © 1985. IMAGE 4 *Trace* (1996); Molissa Fenley in performance at the Joyce Theater, New York; painting by Roy Fowler. Photograph by Julie Lemberger © 1996.

A Chronology of Molissa Fenley's Works

1977

Planets. Premiered at the Merce Cunningham Studio, New York.

1978

The Willies. Performed by Molissa Fenley and Richard Guimond. Premiered at Dance Theater Workshop, New York.

The Cats. Performed by Molissa Fenley, Neil Greenberg and Richard Guimond. Premiered at the Merce Cunningham Studio, New York.

1979

Red Art Screen. Performed by Molissa Fenley and Joan Frost; video by Keith Haring (live version). Premiered at the School of Visual Arts, New York.

Mix. Performed by John Bernd, Molissa Fenley, Kate McLaughlin and Elizabeth Streb; costumes by Carmel Johnson. Commissioned by and premiered at the Kitchen, New York.

Video Clones. Video by Keith Haring

1980

Boca Raton. Performed by Molissa Fenley and Elizabeth Streb; music by Paul Alexander (loop of *The Talking Heads*); design by Steve Keister. Premiered at the Kitchen, New York.

Energizer. Performed by Lynne Allard, Molissa Fenley, Pat Graf and Susanna Weiss; music by Mark Freedman; costumes by Yasha and Yonson Pak; lighting by Philip Sandstrom. Commissioned by and premiered at Dance Theater Workshop, New York.

1981

Peripheral Vision. Performed by Molissa Fenley; music by Mark Freedman; costume by Yonson Pak; lighting by Philip Sandstrom. Commissioned by and premiered at the American Dance Festival, Durham, NC.

Gentle Desire. Performed by Lynne Allard, Demi Bank and Molissa Fenley; music by Mark Freedman; costumes by Yonson Pak; lighting by Philip Sandstrom. Commissioned by and premiered at the American Dance Festival, Durham, NC.

1982

Eureka. Performed by Molissa Fenley; music by Peter Gordon; costumes by Yonson Pak; lighting by Philip Sandstrom. Commissioned by and premiered at Dance Theater Workshop, New York.

1983

Hemispheres. Performed by Molissa Fenley, Silvia Martins and Scottie Mirviss; visual element by Francesco Clemente; music by Anthony Davis; costumes by Rei Kawakubo; lighting by Kathy Kaufman. Commissioned by and premiered at the Brooklyn Academy of Music's Next Wave Festival, New York.

1985

Esperanto. Performed by Elizabeth Benjamin, Jill Diamond, Molissa Fenley, Silvia Martins and Scottie Mirviss; music by Ryuichi Sakamoto; costumes by Jean-Paul Gaultier; lighting by Gary Mintz. Commissioned by Tsurumoto Room, Tokyo; premiered at the Endo Memorial Hall, Tokyo.

Cenotaph. Performed by Elizabeth Benjamin, Jill Diamond, Molissa Fenley, Silvia Martins and Scottie Mirviss; music by Jamaaladeen Tacuma; text by Eric Bogosian; lighting by Gary Mintz. Commissioned by and premiered at Jacob's Pillow Dance Festival, Beckett, MA.

1986

Feral. Performed by the Ohio Ballet; music by Robert Lloyd. Commissioned by and premiered at the Ohio Ballet, Akron, OH.

Geologic Moments. Performed by Molissa Fenley, Douglas Johnson, Silvia Martins, Christopher Mattox and Scottie Mirviss; music by Philip Glass and Julius Eastman; costumes by Sandi Fellman; lighting by Gary Mintz. Commissioned by and premiered at the Brooklyn Academy of Music's Next Wave Festival, New York.

A Descent into the Maelstrom. Performed by the Australian Dance Theatre; music by Philip Glass; direction by Matthew McGuire; design by Eamon D'Arcy. Commissioned by and premiered at the Adelaide Festival, Adelaide, Australia.

1987

Separate Voices. Performed by Molissa Fenley, Douglas Johnson, Silvia Martins, Robert Mason and Scottie Mirviss; costumes by Sandi Fellman; lighting by David Moodey. Commissioned by and premiered at the Joyce Theater, New York.

1988

In Recognition. Performed by Molissa Fenley; music by Philip Glass; lighting by David Moodey. Commissioned by and premiered at Serious Fun, Lincoln Center for the Performing Arts, New York.

State of Darkness. Performed by Molissa Fenley; music by Igor Stravinsky (*Le Sacre du Printemps*); lighting by David Moodey. Commissioned by and premiered at the American Dance Festival, Durham, NC. Performed by Peter Boal in 1999 (commissioned by Lincoln Center Out-of-Doors Festival); performed by the Pacific Northwest Ballet in 2007 (alternately performed by Rachel Foster, James Moore and Jonathan Porretta); revived by the Pacific Northwest Ballet in 2014 (alternately performed by Angelica Generosa, James Moore, Jonathan Porretta and Matthew Renko).

1989

Augury. Performed by Molissa Fenley and Doug Varone; music by Christopher Hyams-Hart; choreography in collaboration with Doug Varone. Commissioned by and premiered at the American Dance Festival, Durham, NC.

The Floor Dances. Performed by Molissa Fenley; sculpture by Richard Long; music by Henryk Gorecki; lighting by David Moodey. Commissioned by and premiered at the Dia Art Foundation, New York.

Provenance Unknown. Performed by Molissa Fenley; music by Philip Glass; costume by Sandi Fellman; lighting by David Moodey. Commissioned by and premiered at Dance Chance, Dance Theater Workshop, New York.

1990

Bardo. Performed by Molissa Fenley; music by Somei Satoh. Commissioned by Jacob's Pillow Dance Festival; premiered at the Keith Haring Memorial, St John the Divine, New York.

1991

Inner Enchantments. Performed by Molissa Fenley; music by Philip Glass; lighting by David Moodey. Commissioned by and premiered at the Joyce Theater, New York.

1992

Place. Performed by Molissa Fenley; music by Arvo Part; costumes by Gabriel Berry; lighting by David Moodey. Commissioned by and premiered at the Joyce Theater, New York.

Threshold. Performed by Molissa Fenley; music by Arvo Part; costumes by Gabriel Berry; lighting by David Moodey. Premiered at the Joyce Theater, New York.

1993

Escalay. Performed by Molissa Fenley and Christopher Mattox; music by Hamza el Din; costumes by Gabriel Berry; lighting by David Moodey. Premiered at the Kitchen, New York.

Tilliboyo. Performed by Molissa Fenley; music by Foday Musa Suso; costume by Gabriel Berry; lighting by David Moodey. Premiered at the Kitchen, New York.

Sightings. Performed by Molissa Fenley; sculpture by Tatsuo Miyajima; music by Pauline Oliveros; costume by Gabriel Berry; lighting by Jan Kroeze. Commissioned by and premiered at the Joyce Theater, New York.

Nullarbor. Performed by Molissa Fenley; sculpture by Richard Long; music by Robert Lloyd; costume by Gabriel Berry; lighting by Jan Kroeze. Premiered at the Joyce Theater, New York.

Channel. Performed by Molissa Fenley; sculpture by Richard Serra; music by Somei Satoh; costume by Gabriel Berry; lighting by Jan Kroeze. Premiered at the Joyce Theater, New York.

Witches' Float. Performed by Molissa Fenley; sculpture by Kiki Smith; music by Alvin Lucier; costume by Gabriel Berry. Commissioned by and premiered at the Krannert Art Center, Urbana-Champaign, IL.

1994

Bridge of Dreams. Performed by the Deutsche Oper Ballett; sculpture by Kiki Smith; music by Laurie Anderson; costumes by Gabriel Berry; lighting by Robert Wierzel. Commissioned and premiered at the Deutsche Oper, Berlin.

Jalan Jalan. Performed by Molissa Fenley; music by Lou Harrison; costume by Gabriel Berry. Premiered at Indonesian International Dance Festival, Jakarta.

1995

Sita. Performed by Molissa Fenley and Paz Tanjuaquio in alternation; photography by Sandi Fellman; music by Philip Glass; costumes by Gabriel Berry; lighting by David Moodey. Commissioned by and premiered at the Joyce Theater, New York.

Savanna. Performed by Peggy Baker; music by Peter Garland; costume by Gabriel Berry; lighting by David Moodey. Commissioned by Peggy Baker Projects and premiered at the 92Y, New York.

1996

Latitudes. A work created for the Internet, www.diaart.org/Fenley

Pola'a. Performed by Molissa Fenley, alternately by Peter Boal; music by Lou Harrison; costumes by Evan Ayotte; lighting by David Moodey. Commissioned by and premiered at Jacob's Pillow Dance Festival, New York. Subsequently reconfigured as a duet, performed by Peter Boal and Molissa Fenley (commissioned by and premiered at the New National Theater, Tokyo).

1997

Trace. Performed by Molissa Fenley, text read by Jane Smith; painting by Roy Fowler; music by Jonathan Hart Makwaia; text by John Jesurun; lighting by David Moodey. Commissioned by and premiered at the Joyce Theater, New York.

Icho. Performed by Felicia Norton; music by Leroy Jenkins; costume by Gabriel Berry. Commissioned by Felicia Norton; premiered at Lincoln Center Out-of-Doors Festival, New York.

On the Other Ocean. Performed by Molissa Fenley; music by David Behrman; costume by Gabriel Berry; lighting by David Moodey. Commissioned by and premiered at Summerstage, New York.

1998

La Muse Menagere. Performed by Molissa Fenley; music by Darius Milhaud. Commissioned by and premiered at the Littlefield Concert Hall, Mills College, Oakland, CA.

Tala. Performed by Molissa Fenley; music by John Cage; lighting by David Moodey. Premiered at Dia Art Foundation, New York.

1999

Timbral Inventions. Performed by dancers of the University of Utah, Salt Lake City; music by John Cage; lighting by David Moodey. Commissioned by the University of Utah, Salt Lake City; premiered at the Lincoln Center Out-of-Doors Festival, New York.

Voices. Performed by Molissa Fenley; music by Kevin Volans, as performed by Joan Jeanrenaud; lighting by David Moodey. Premiered at Theatre Artaud, San Francisco.

2000

Island. Performed by Molissa Fenley; sculpture by Carol Hepper; music by Harold Meltzer; lighting by David Moodey. Premiered at the Kitchen, New York.

Weathering. Performed by Molissa Fenley; sculpture by Merrill Wagner; lighting by David Moodey. Premiered at the Kitchen, New York.

Ceremony. Performed by Molissa Fenley; text by Joy Harjo; Premiered at Lafayette College, Easton, PA.

Spring Waterfall. Performed by Molissa Fenley; music by Philip Glass and Foday Musa Suso. Premiered at Lafayette College, Easton, PA.

I and You Resemble Each Other, Now. Performed by dancers of the University of Utah, Salt Lake City. Premiered at the University of Utah, Salt Lake City.

Delta. Performed by Molissa Fenley, Paz Tanjuaquio and Heather Waldon; music by John Cage; lighting by David Moodey. Commissioned by and premiered at the Joyce Theater, New York.

2001

Folds. Performed by Molissa Fenley and Bebe Miller; music by Fred Frith; choreography in collaboration with Bebe Miller. Commissioned by and premiered at Virginia Commonwealth University, Richmond, VA.

Signs/Landmark. Performed by Peter Boal and Molissa Fenley; music by Lou Harrison for *Signs*; music by Somei Satoh for *Landmark*, as played by Aki Takahashi. Commissioned by and premiered at the New National Theater, Tokyo.

2002

331 Steps. Performed by Leslie Braithwaite, Molissa Fenley and Paz Tanjuaquio; visual design by Merrill Wagner; music by Laetitia

Sonami; costumes by Evan Ayotte; lighting by David Moodey. Commissioned by and premiered at the Joyce Theater, New York.

Short Stories. Performed by Leslie Braithwaite, Nora Chipaumire, Ori Flomin, Linda Sastradiprajda and Paz Tanjuaquio, in silence; costumes by Chado, Ralph Rucci. Premiered at the Joyce Theater, New York.

2003

Waiting for Rain. Performed by Peter Boal; music by Robert Ashley; design by Roy Fowler; costume by Mark Zappone. Commissioned by Peter Boal; premiered at the Joyce Theater, New York.

Water Courses. Performed by Ashley Brunning, Kate Dunn, Molissa Fenley, Wanjiru Kamuyu and Cassie Mey; music and text by Joy Harjo. Premiered at Joyce Soho, New York.

Kuro Shio. Performed by dancers of Women in Dance, Seoul / Tokyo; music by Bun-Ching Lam. Commissioned by and premiered at the National Theater, Seoul.

2004

Lava Field. Performed by Ashley Brunning, Molissa Fenley, Wanjiru Kamuyu and Cassie Mey; music by John Bischoff; costumes by Khadda. Premiered at the Joyce Theater, New York.

2005

Patterns and Expectations. Performed by Ashley Brunning, Molissa Fenley, Wanjiru Kamuyu and Cassie Mey; music by Fred Frith; costumes by Evan Ayotte. Premiered at Joyce Soho, New York.

Desert Sea. Performed by Repertory Dance Theater; music by Lou Harrison; costumes by Khadda. Commissioned by and premiered at Repertory Dance Theater, Salt Lake City, UT.

2006

Dreaming Awake. Performed by Molissa Fenley; music by Philip Glass. Commissioned by and premiered at the Rovereto Music Festival, Italy.

Four Lines. Performed by Molissa Fenley; music by Jon Gibson. Premiered at Allentown Symphony Hall, Allentown, PA.

2007

Calculus and Politics. Performed by Eric Bradley, Ashley Brunning, Katie McGreevy, Cassie Mey, Luke Miller, Paul Singh and Dusan Tynek; music by Harry Partch; costumes by Khadda. Commissioned by and premiered at the Joyce Theater, New York.

Castor. Performed by the Seattle Dance Project; music by Harry Partch; costumes by Mark Zappone. Commissioned by and premiered by Seattle Dance Project, Seattle, WA.

2008

Cosmati Variations 1–4. Performed by Stefania Biffani, Molissa Fenley, Elisabetta Minutoli and Marco Rodontini; music by John Cage. Premiered at the American Academy in Rome, Italy.

2009

Ice, Dew, Food, Crew, Ape. Performed by Molissa Fenley, Katie McGreevy, Cassie Mey, Karin Stevens, Paz Tanjuaquio and Alyssa Wilmot; music by Alvin Curran with John Cage, soloist, and the ship horn of the Nantucket Light Ship II, and poem *Step* by Bob Holman. Premiered at the Atlantic Center for the Arts, New Smyrna Beach, FL.

Mass Balance. Performed by Molissa Fenley; music by Cenk Ergun; prop by Todd Richmond. Premiered at Theater Artaud, San Francisco.

Double Beginning. In collaboration with Bob Holman. Subsequently reconfigured as a trio for Molissa Fenley, Cassie Mey and Katie McGreevy and premiered in March 2010 at 92Y, New York.

2010

94 Feathers. Performed by Molissa Fenley, Katie McGreevy and Cassie Mey; props by Merrill Wagner; music by Cenk Ergun; costumes by Jill St Coeur; lighting by David Moodey. Premiered at the 92Y, New York.

Planes in Air. Performed by Molissa Fenley, Katie McGreevy and Cassie Mey; props by Roy Fowler; music by Joan Jeanrenaud; costumes by Jill St Coeur; lighting by David Moodey. Premiered at the 92Y, New York.

Pieces of Land. Performed by Molissa Fenley, Katie McGreevy and Cassie Mey; props by Jene Highstein; music by Jason Hoopes; costumes by Jill St Coeur; lighting by David Moodey. Premiered at the 92Y, New York.

Prop Dance #5. Performed by Molissa Fenley, Katie McGreevy and Cassie Mey; props by Keith Sonnier; music by Lainie Fefferman; costumes by Jill St Coeur; lighting by David Moodey. Premiered at the 92Y, New York.

Regions—Chair, *Ocean Walk*, *Mesa* (*Revival*). Performed by Molissa Fenley, Katie McGreevy and Cassie Mey; music by Maggi Payne; set by Roy Fowler; costume reconstruction by Jeffrey Wirsing; original lighting by David Moodey. Premiered at the 92Y, New York.

2011

The Vessel Stories. Performed by Molissa Fenley, Cassie Mey and Cassandra Neville; music by Philip Glass; costumes by Jill St Coeur. Commissioned by and premiered at Geoffrey Hendricks' The Art Barn, Colindale, Cape Breton, Nova Scotia. Subsequently reconfigured as a quartet with dancer Peiling Kao and premiered at the Days and Nights Festival, Carmel, CA.

Credo in Us. Performed by Molissa Fenley, Garth Grimball, Cassie Mey, Katherine McGinity, Cuauhtemoc Peranda, Judene Small and Alyssa Wilmot; music by John Cage. Commissioned by and premiered at the Mills College Art Museum, Oakland, CA.

2012

Cross Bridge. Performed by Holley Farmer, Molissa Fenley and Rosemary Quinn; in collaboration with Holley Farmer, John Jesurun, David Moodey and Rosemary Quinn; costumes by Juanita Cardenas. Premiere at La Mama, New York.

Found Object (solo version). Performed by Molissa Fenley. Premiered at the Basilica, Hudson, NY.

2013

Energizer. Performed by Christiana Axelsen, Rebecca Chaleff, Molissa Fenley, Peiling Kao and Cassandra Neville; reconstructed from the original recording of the opening in 1980; music by Mark Freedman; costume reconstruction by Jill St Coeur; lighting by David Moodey. Performed at New York Live Arts, New York.

Dance an Impossible Space. Performed by Molissa Fenley; projections by Jean-Pierre Giovanelli; music by Flavio Perenda. Premiered at the Chalet, Bogliasco Foundation, Bogliasco, Italy.

Found Object. Performed by Christiana Axelsen, Rebecca Chaleff, Molissa Fenley, Peiling Kao and Rosemary Quinn; instructions contributed by John Guare, Joy Harjo and Rudy Wurlitzer; music by Erin Gee; additional choreography by Rebecca Chaleff, Peiling Kao and Rosemary Quinn; props by Jene Highstein; paintings by Roy Fowler; costumes by Ada Hatcher. Premiered at New York Live Arts, New York.

Witches' Float. Performed by Holley Farmer; reconstructed by Molissa Fenley; music by Alvin Lucier; sculpture by Kiki Smith; costume reconstruction by Jill St Coeur. Performed at New York Live Arts, New York.

2014

BEAMS. Performed by Christiana Axelsen, Rebecca Chaleff, Peiling Kao with dancers from Mills College; music by Alvin Curran. Premiered at the Mills College Art Museum, Oakland, CA.

Entrance. Performed by Christiana Axelsen and Molissa Fenley; music by David Behrman; costume by Yumiko. Premiered at the Flea, New York.

Esperanto. Performed by Christiana Axelsen, Rebecca Chaleff, Evan Flood and Matthew Roberts; reconstructed by Christiana Axelsen and Molissa Fenley; music by Ryuichi Sakamoto. Performed at the Judson Memorial Church, New York.

Redwood Park, Part 1. Performed by Victor Chavez, Evan Flood, Emily Kerr, Marte Madera and Matthew Roberts; music by Joan Jeanrenaud; performed live by Nava Dunkelman and Anna Wray; costumes by Christopher Dunn. Commissioned and premiered by the Oakland Ballet, Oakland, CA.

Redwood Park, Part 2. Performed by Christiana Axelsen, Rebecca Chaleff, Evan Flood and Matthew Roberts. Premiered at the Judson Memorial Church, New York.

Dance an Impossible Space. Performed by Christiana Axelsen, Rebecca Chaleff and Molissa Fenley; music by Erin Gee; costumes by Jill St Coeur. Premiered at the Judson Memorial Church, New York.

2015

On the Other Ocean. Performed by Christiana Axelsen, Rebecca Chaleff, Molissa Fenley; music by David Behrman; costumes by Jill St Coeur. Premiered at the Mills College Art Museum, Oakland, CA.

Foreword

I was drawn to Molissa Fenley and her work from the moment I saw her and what must have been her first dance company. The performance took place at the Kitchen, then a centre for music and dance located on Broome Street. These were the emerging years of the 1970s when New York's Soho was home to new ideas in dance, theatre, music and art. Partly a neighbourhood of 'sweat shops' and small factories, the transition, though, to artists' lofts, galleries and music/dance performance spaces was on in full swing. The floors of these new studios often bore the marks left by rows of sewing machines that used to fill those industrial lofts. In those years, on most evenings in the spring, summer, autumn and winter, anyone strolling through the then-empty streets could, and often did, hear the sounds of music, dance and theatre performances floating from open loft windows high above as well as from street-level storefronts turned into makeshift theatres.

Robert Wilson, Richard Foreman, The Wooster Group, Jonas Mekas' Cinematheque; dancers/performers Trisha Brown, Yvonne Rainer, Steve Paxton; musicians La Monte Young, Steve Reich and Terry Riley; Meredith Monk (wearing as many artistic 'hats' as she could); and I—and many, many more—all began to fill in those emptying spaces.

So New York's sweat shops hadn't gone away at all. Same shops, different sweat.

And our artistic parents were there too—John Cage, Merce Cunningham, Bob Rauschenberg, Jasper Johns and, again, many,

many others. They were there—and not as a mere presence. By making their work there as well, they were a blessing and inspiration to us all.

That was where I first saw Molissa. The energy of her work was as clear and as strong as it is today. It goes without saying that it was, and continues to be, immediately addictive for the spectators. You would go to see Mo (as she is known to us) for your dance/music energy 'fix'. And it would stay with you for all of that night, if not for days afterwards. The vigour and innovation of her constantly appearing inventions kept the young and not-so-young audiences coming back for more. And there has always been more on the way.

Thanks to her artistic vision, stamina and commitment to the highest standards of her art, she and her work remain alive, well and with us to this day. Short of knowing and seeing her work, this book will give you a glimpse, and an important one, of her and the artistic visions that drive her.

For me, having been part of her work as a collaborator and dedicated follower has been one of the joys of my personal and professional lives.

Philip Glass
18 February 2013

IMAGE 5 *Hemispheres* (1983); Molissa Fenley, photo session in New York; costume by Rei Kawakubo. Photograph by Robert Mapplethorpe © 1983.

IMAGE 6 *Gentle Desire* (1982); in performance at Teatro Nuovo, Naples, Italy. Photograph by Enzo Esposito © 1982.

Watching a Friend Becoming

Bill T. Jones

I suppose it could be said that a discussion of anyone's choreographic work is a series of encounters recalled. It is a process that is certainly imperfect, but it is the way I have chosen to speak about this remarkable woman, my friend Molissa Fenley. There is no overarching conclusion to be drawn. I offer these recollections, these sightings, as nothing more than mementos.

When did I first see Molissa? I believe it was in 1979 when I attended a performance of *Mix*, an early work, at the Kitchen Center for Video, Music and Dance. And again shortly afterwards, in 1980, at Dance Theater Workshop, I saw what became an early signature work, *Energizer,* a quartet in this particular permutation as I recall. Molissa was of medium height, with the muscularity and confidence of a professional athlete. Her energy seemed boundless—it was only Molissa who could have taken a pop-advertising concept generally associated with batteries and an unstoppable rabbit and made a serious study of human locomotion and the heightened consciousness experienced by people operating at maximum physical exertion over long periods of time.

What was the vocabulary?

Molissa was taking the concept of minimalism as our generation had inherited it from the likes of Donald Judd, Carl Andre, Sol Lewitt, Lucinda Childs and Laura Dean and weighed in as the 'postmodern' era's latest expression of this concept of repetition shorn of psychological and theatrical trappings, where all her movement was stripped down to its frank essentials. Much of the vocabulary was recognizable, but with a difference: there were endless runs that became *jetés* that would unexpectedly shift direction at their apex. There were windmill arms like propellers projecting from the pulled-up, pulsing ribcage. There were skipping patterns followed by the three dancers, often in unison, criss-crossing the space, forming lines, circles, triangles and other geometric configurations more sensed than read. The costumes were one of the most peculiar and effective I have ever seen—their charm lay in their off-hand, improvised construction out of the cheapest polyester fabric in outrageous colours (was it hot pink, lime green, maybe orange?) that changed shades as the dancers' sweat soaked their armpits, their sternums, the space between their shoulder blades, the small of their back, their crotches.

Molissa, with a pair of full lips that would have been the envy of a young movie starlet, had allure and sensuality; she was accompanied by an equally fierce-spirited, sexy Elizabeth Streb, who would go on to make her own foray into that place where extreme focus, energy and courage meet; and John Bernd—an associate director of Dance Space—a leading practitioner of the 'new dance', who would make striking works exploring gay identity with performance artist Tim Miller. (Bernd would be one of the first people in the downtown scene to go public with his HIV status, dying of AIDS in 1988.)

The next time I encountered Molissa was at the Moderna Museet in Stockholm as she and her partner Lynne Allard were finishing a run-through of their shared evening with the great composer–performer Julius Eastman. She and Julius, Arnie Zane and I were sharing an evening with George Lewis and Douglas Ewart, among others, in what was a historic tour sponsored by the Kitchen. My impression of the moment is a recollection not so much of their movements as of what Molissa was like in rehearsal and at rest—something like a lovely pony in full lather. Gracious in greeting me but eager to get back to what she was truly engaged in—those inexhaustible movement sequences.

She, Arnie and I liked—or should I say, were impressed by?—one another immediately, although our styles of movement and personalities were quite different. In 1981, Molissa and I, along with Charlie Moulton, Marlene Pennison and Johanna Boyce, were invited to create new works for the 'Emerging Choreographers' series, as part of the American Dance Festival (recently relocated to Durham, North Carolina, from New London, Connecticut). Checking online, I see that Molissa was performing a work called *Gentle Desire.* Until then I had known Molissa as a dancing athlete with boundless energy, operating at high levels of speed and exertion. Was this the moment when I first saw, or sensed, her palette expanding? Because now there was a new focus placed on extension—lush *arabesque*s, attitude turns, sculpted arms, regally arched spines revelling in the pleasure of carving space as opposed to exploding it.

Was it around then that Molissa and I developed the pleasant ritual of her inviting me to see her rehearsing her latest work? Excited and moved to be alone with her and her process, I began to see the depth of her commitment to a life in dance. I began to really understand the daily discipline of getting oneself to the studio—often alone, prepared physically and mentally and then fashioning something through all sorts of critical, financial and emotional climates. It was there that I began to see what it really meant to 'do the work as a way of life'.

The years and the sightings stream by and blur.

Molissa with *Hemispheres* (music by Anthony Davis) at the Brooklyn Academy of Music's Next Wave Festival. The music was jazz-inflected classical, not necessarily driven by a pulse. At that time, all of us 'emerging choreographers' were evermore involved in crossover collaborations with the visual world. So Molissa had asked one of the then-reigning new figurative painters, Francesco Clemente, to collaborate with her. Clemente did not make a three-dimensional decor for the stage but a series of drawings of dismembered female bodies to be inserted in each programme. It was a curious, violent and, perhaps, mocking answer to her request. I always thought that, through those rough, vaguely erotic, decapitated, armless, legless torsos, he was confronting a paragon of physical strength and commitment with a sort of sadistic memento mori.

One of those intimate times with Molissa, at the old Dia rehearsal space on Mercer Street in Soho, as she rehearsed was her deeply felt homage to the Exxon Valdez oil spill. The music, the unbridled meditation on mourning by Henryk Gorecki. After the run-through, she sat with me amid Richard Long's stone-floor piece, *Dancing Stone Circle*, and her measured tone could barely suppress the sadness at the image of birds and other creatures covered in oil and attempting to rise from the muck and devastation.

Her *State of Darkness*—was it the same rehearsal?—set to Igor Stravinsky's *Rite of Spring* holds a special place in the sightings. Arnie Zane had died not too long before, and she expressed to me that there was something of him—and me also?—in the motif that set her bare chest fluttering in terror, hyperventilating, with expectation or dread, at the thought of some ordeal she must face. We were all raw at that time from the ravages of the HIV epidemic. Some of us were dead or dying; some of us were observing; and some of us were trying to give it a name, a face. In Molissa's case, it was bearing witness through her robust, tenacious body.

Another of those rehearsals when she showed me a work, *Bardo*, that was upright, restrained and so clear in its space and gesture that I actually asked her if I could learn it. We were both very excited by the prospect, though I am sorry to say it never materialized.

Esperanto was a repertory piece that she set on my company as we were preparing for our December 1993 season at the Joyce Theater. This was probably the most difficult time I ever had with her work. It was difficult for several reasons: I felt that the peculiar pitch of her hyper-physicality demanded a kind of detachment that my dancers—Odile Reine Adelaide, Maia Saffrin and, most incongruously, Arthur Aviles—would not be suited for. It was extremely complicated and, as a result, difficult to learn, needing more time than I had anticipated as I myself was designing a very ambitious series of new works and revivals. I found myself competing with her for my own dancers and their energy. Also, *Esperanto*'s protracted length made it very difficult to programme with other items from my company's repertory. It was a difficult time in our friendship, but, as a testament to her graciousness and our care for each other, no irreparable damage was done.

I was not at the Joyce for the opening-night performance when Molissa's knee was severely injured and she had to cancel the entire engagement. We didn't see each other for a while. If I remember correctly, though, the next time we were together was in one of her intimate showings that she shared with me. Once again I was astounded at the focus, discipline and determination that had allowed her to physically, mentally and metaphorically pull herself back on her feet with new works and a heroic rethinking of her movements informed by necessity.

And finally, seeing *Hemispheres* restaged at the Kitchen with Anthony Davis and his band, playing his eponymous composition, after over 20 years, was at once deeply moving and challenging. Moving, because we were all older and the work in its original incarnation had been such an original expression of a young woman's determination and ambition. Challenging, because it asked questions about the nature of a life in dance. The athletic, muscular and brash individual I had first seen over 20 years before was gone; in her place stood a much thinner, wiry and naked presence exuding a generosity that comes from suffering and survivorship. But here was Molissa still 'carving space', organizing the other dancers, even the music, around something serene, steadfast and hard won.

These above sightings are distressingly incomplete, vague and imprecise.

Molissa, like me, continues, and by doing so helps to answer the question of what is a life given to the stage, to this frustrating ritual called dancing that so many of us love . . .

There is a truth and an affirmation here, a creed—faith through persistence and persistence in faith.

IMAGES 7–8 *94 Feathers* (*The Prop Dances*) (2010); Molissa Fenley, Katie McGreevy, Cassie Mey in performance at Joyce Soho, New York; set by Merrill Wagner. Photographs by Julie Lemberger © 2010.

Walking with Molissa Fenley

Ann Murphy

> I have told you, the whole life span of a human is a journey. What we are doing now is a journey. All movements are journeys. We are progressing, we are moving.
>
> Ositola, Yoruban Diviner (quoted in Drewal 1992: 47)

Two summers ago, I went east to New York to comb through Molissa Fenley's video archives at Lincoln Center Library for the Performing Arts, looking for clues to explain the choreographer's mysterious post-modern dances. Molissa had been the 'bad girl' of the downtown scene in the 1980s, her sleek boyish frame, spiky short hair, hungry hands, blunt feet and regal spine giving her an air of elegant rebelliousness. But more than the way she looked, it was the way she moved—with a radically new ferocity—that distinguished her from her peers. When she bolted across space, she seemed to set the stage on fire, flying through various landscapes, real or imaginary, for extreme stretches of time. Her laser-like intensity, her drive, laced the work with mystery. But what exactly that mystery was eluded me. I hoped to understand it better with a closer look.

I spent part of my week in the city in front of one of Lincoln Center library's video monitors, then headed down below Canal Street to meet Molissa at her office at the old 1896 American Thread Building, once home to the Wool Exchange, where today hard-working well-known performing artists have offices on the ground floor and plush millionaires have swank apartments on the floors above. Those were hot, breezy July days—the sun laid itself like a fat spatula against the skin and the summer air was already dense and sticky. Wending my way through the building's cool rotunda, I passed into a hall and then angled down a second, shorter corridor before entering through the last door. There I discovered a large L-shaped space with a separate, walled-off office facing Broadway. That far room was Mimi Johnson's, the visionary arts administrator who shepherds Momenta Foundation, Molissa's non-profit, and who over the years has managed the careers of such avant-garde composers as John Cage, David Tudor, Robert Ashley, Alvin Lucier, Philip Glass and Gordon Mumma, among others. While she once had a stable of performing artists to complement musicians like Ashley, she shed all but Molissa and avant-garde theatre director Richard Foreman.

As I looked around, I saw CDs stacked high on an army of metal bookshelves. The air conditioner groaned ineffectively, and, through a couple of large windows in Mimi's office, I saw New Yorkers swim by as though in a cloudy fishbowl. Molissa was hard at work, typing precisely on a computer keyboard. When I settled in, I noticed that she seemed visually bound to the computer terminal—her erect body was wholly balanced, poised, unmoving, not even twitching, and performing an intense labour that lasted for about an hour as she kept hard at various tasks. I sat at a round table nearby, going through old newspaper clippings to find out what New York critics had said 30 years ago. I was fidgety while Molissa sat with Zen poise. Suddenly, like cannon shot, she bolted out of her chair. 'Let's go for a coffee,' she said, already in action, her large black traveller's wallet in her hand. I scrambled for my bag and followed in her wake, dashing with her across the street for iced coffee at a bakery run by a sweet young man sporting a vast tangle of dreadlocks. But we didn't linger. Five minutes later, we were back in the office for another round of work, she hammering out a grant proposal, me scouring through old clippings. But this stint was briefer: less than an hour passed before Molissa needed to move again. She was in earnest—we would take a walk.

Molissa—who is 5 foot 5, 100 pounds and as lithe and muscular as a woman from some distant highland—has a potent need to move, and so we began an excursion heading west, towards the Hudson River. She planned to show me where she and her tall, and equally lithe, husband Roy had seen the fireworks the night before. We headed to the esplanade built along the river before the attacks of 9/11. We set out at a clip and I soon realized that this was no ordinary walk. I examined the cobbles as we rushed past, wondered about the age of the large stone buildings and made mental notes to look up the location of the various streams that had coursed through this part of the island into the eighteenth century, before the canals were filled in or covered over. But there was no time to ponder—it was all I could do to keep up with Molissa's athletic stride, since our progression was less a walk than a slow jog. Soon I could feel the canvas of my black Chuck Ts rubbing against my bare heels; the wounds that were forming began to weep. I wondered how long this excursion would last. More critically, I thought, how long would I?

I turned my eyes to Molissa and watched as she moved without letting up, without slackening her pace. As I worked to keep up, a delicate sheen of sweat coated my skin, like a slick of water glistening on a San Francisco seal, even though I knew I shared none of the seal's damp glory. I watched as Molissa dodged a slow-poke pedestrian—she appeared to push forward effortlessly. Her cotton blouse billowed in a wind created by her speed, and she shimmered and vibrated, cool, unruffled. From the pleasure on her face as she met each new volume of air, I could see how space and motion thrilled her. Energy seemed to swell out and fill the region around her body, charging the atmosphere, creating the sense that she was projecting herself forward into time, like a musician playing at the front edge of a note, transforming energy into momentum and momentum into action in a kind of physics of the spirit. It made sense that she named her non-profit entity Momenta—the plural of momentum, a force essential to even glacial progress, it captures her love of bodies moving along clear vectors.

This energy emanating from her called to mind something Frieda Lawrence had once said about D. H. Lawrence, her husband: '[H]is bond with everything in creation is so amazing, no preconceived ideas, just a meeting between him and a creature, a tree, a cloud, anything [. . .]. I call it love, but it is something else [. . .] "saying yes"' (quoted in Dyer 1997: 111–12). As Molissa was enlivening her surroundings on that sultry day, open to 'a creature, a tree, a cloud', I realized that she was meeting the world with a similar emphatic yes and transmitting back what Henri Bergson calls *élan vital* or creative life force, what the Yorubans call *ase*. It manifests as power, intelligence, will and an awakened and laser-like focus. It is what anthropologist Margaret Thompson Drewal describes as 'the power to bring things into existence' or 'to make things happen' (1992: *xix*). I noted that most of the rest of us, by contrast, seemed to be slogging along in a hazy dream. As I pondered this disparity between her and the general population, I had a growing sense that Molissa's upbringing had something crucial to do with what, at heart, seemed a phenomenological divide.

In 1961, when Molissa was six, her father made a decision to move the whole family to Nigeria. Although he was then a professor of agriculture at Cornell University, Molissa's mother, Eileen, suffered from multiple sclerosis, and the disease was progressing rapidly. Doctors recommended that the family go somewhere warm, since the medical profession believed at the time that a hot climate could help retard the disease. This was during the early days of President John F. Kennedy's administration, when the US had recently instituted the United States Agency for International Development (USAID), and, being adventurous and socially motivated, her parents joined the governmental ranks in Africa so that Professor Fenley could teach what were understood to be best farming practices to Nigerian farmers in the bush. He had come from the high-desert farming community of Hemet outside Riverside, California; Eileen's family had migrated from England to Canada when she was young. They found the idea of uprooting themselves and landing somewhere new both familiar and appealing.

Molissa was the youngest of three children, and the transition to Africa was abrupt and frightening at first. But she adapted to her new surroundings with a swiftness that surprised even her. The beauty of the city of Ibadan, a bustling third-world metropolis of improvised buildings, markets and celebrations, and the extensive physical freedom that allowed her to be at large and roam the land, connected her back to what she describes as early ecstatic experiences of nature while in New York. She still remembers the day when she looked up at the beauty of the blue Ithaca sky and found herself overcome with a feeling of bliss. Nigeria, where experience was heightened by the intensity of the dense landscape, offered that tenfold. Molissa quickly became attuned to a nature that was prolific, mysterious and timeless as well as time-bound, and filled, she thought, with palpable but unseen forces. Outside school—a rigorous British-run enterprise—she ran about without shirt or shoes, and spent her non-school hours largely alone or exploring with her brother Rick the countryside where they taught themselves to perceive and understand nature with great acuity. Molissa became a fearless young explorer, unfazed by threats of parasites or poisonous snakes. The bush became her country.

> I remember . . . feeling very proprietary about the whole place . . . . There were so many moments of bliss . . . of seeing beautiful relationships of tree boughs against the sky, against tall grass, against vines, and against the beautiful red earth . . . . It was geometrically very beautiful too.

> [The bush paths ran through] deep rain forest . . . roots everywhere . . . rain everywhere . . . mud everywhere, and vines . . . . It was really jungle [with] beautiful palm trees, all sorts of animals—not big-game animals—but all sorts of birds and snakes and lizards, beautiful sounds, strange insects [that propel you] . . . into a heightened auditory sense . . . .
>
> There were these green mambas that would hang down from the tree boughs . . . and obviously you would not walk beneath them. That would be very problematic. You'd just become aware that things had . . . a . . . way of being, and when that way of being was in some way disrupted, then you had to watch out . . . .[1]

Southwestern Nigeria is home to the ancient kingdom of Yorubaland, a colonial designation of a complex, linguistically linked group of 25 million people, and includes areas of Benin and Togo to the west. It is believed to have consolidated in the seventh century BCE and became one of the great African cultures, known for its philosophy, art, oral tradition, ritual and craftsmanship. By 1900, it was colonized by the British after centuries of control by the Portuguese, the Dutch and the French. By the 1960s, oil was a great colonial magnet and drew governments from around the world to the petroleum trade or the ancillary activities of national development and political brokering. This meant that children of international governmental and non-governmental workers, children like Molissa, filled the Senior Staff School in Ibadan, a city 73 miles inland from the Gulf of Guinea, or at the International School in Lagos, the capital, which sits on the coast.

But Molissa had an advantage few of her peers had—her father's job took him into the countryside and he let Molissa accompany him whenever possible. They had their favourite rest stops, and, inevitably, at one of the clearings, with an air of magic, the scene would shift from them being the only people on the road to being surrounded by 'twenty people . . . selling pineapples . . . . It was like a constant beautiful circus . . . and I don't mean that frivolously. I mean that life was teeming and colourful.'[2] This sense of marvel was not limited to the bush, though—

Yoruban culture overflowed with rich improvised events. Celebration and spectacle were constant occurrences in Ibadan and Lagos, with dance and music unfolding everywhere to mark events large and small. Each visit by a dignitary of any stripe transformed into an occasion for a festival.

> [O]ften in town there'd be these huge celebrations . . . someone would be coming into town—the visiting chief or something—and everyone would be out . . . and . . . [there would be] beautiful dance, and bright lovely colours and that intense singing with that voice that's striated . . . men, women dancing with women, sometimes together. [There was] always . . . a great band playing. It was very beautiful and loud and rhythmic, and I always wanted to join in.[3]

Sometimes during their wanderings, Molissa and Rick would stumble upon ceremonies and spy 'some ritual . . . taking place that we would watch from afar . . . there was something extraordinarily beautiful about these rituals.'[4] While she yearned to interact, and felt it wasn't enough just to watch, these rituals were often private and off bounds. When the ceremonies were public, though, Molissa was able to witness dancing that often lasted hours, dances that had strict forms and layers, that seemed improvisatory and communal while remaining highly individualized. Space and time in these spectacles and celebrations were conceived as sufficiently elastic—witnesses were able to come and go and were organized by rules that in the West we would apply to play or party rather than to fixed performance. Like the sudden circus-like happenings in the bush, these practices were never trivial. Performers, according to Drewal, are 'people of action', action is the expression of *ase*, and performance is both a re-enactment and metaphor of life's journey (1992: 32).

Happily swimming in this culture, Molissa came to understand something fundamental to Yoruban reality—that the visible and the invisible worlds are 'always in close proximity, and both human and other spirits travel back and forth between the two' (ibid.: 26). For eight years, she traipsed bare-chested and barefoot through the bush, watching, marvelling and feeling one with the people around her as they explored the invisible or 'otherworld', as the Yorubans call the spirit realm, in relation to the visible or 'life/world' (ibid.: 20).

The Return

In 1971, Molissa returned to the US to attend college. She chose Mills College in Oakland, California, drawn by the promise of a small all-women's liberal arts institution with a noted dance programme, and comforted by the fact that her sister would be nearby in Santa Cruz. Molissa was 16, and intent on being a dance therapist—she liked to dance and she knew she wanted to help people, although, in truth, she had no idea what Western concert dance was nor what exactly a dance therapist did. Nevertheless, she signed up for modern dance class and, following the instructions in the department catalogue to wear proper attire, she appeared in the studio dressed in a painter's smock. By the second class, she had commandeered a leotard and tights, and, for the next four years, costumed in the regulation uniform, she joined every dance course, often repeating it in a subsequent semester, and appeared in as many classes as her schedule permitted.[5] She trained in the technique of Martha Graham and José Limon and learnt the theories of Louis Horst and Rudolph von Laban, absorbed herself in music, studied science and set to work right away, creating dances that her mentor, Emerita Professor Rebecca Fuller, said were inspired and inventive from the very outset.[6] Doris Dennison, collaborator of John Cage in the 1930s and 40s, was the department's music director, and students danced not only to Bach but also to the experimental sounds of the composers housed across the street in the sprawling music building where Molissa was introduced to avant-garde music, particularly to minimalism. It became the perfect artistic storm for her—she would acquire techniques of Western dance and music structures in California to channel the West African sensibilities she had absorbed during her formative years.

New Music, often called 'minimalism', helped her on her journey. Coming into being in the Bay Area through the efforts of musicians

La Monte Young, Terry Riley, Lou Harrison and Steve Reich, this groundbreaking music of the 1960s and 70s was defined by its tonality, its continuous drones, its additive structures and polyrhythms, owing its sound first to American jazz and ultimately to the young artists' exposure to African or Asian rhythmic forms. Reich, for one, apprenticed himself to master drummers in Ghana while Riley and Young became devotees of the world-renowned north Indian vocalist Pandit Pran Nath (Schwartz 1996: 71, 42). Harrison, who had a significant influence on Molissa when she was an undergraduate, admired Indonesian music to which he had been exposed in high school and pursued "just" intonation, eventually creating his own 'American gamelan orchestra' out of aluminium odds and ends. Reich was spurred on by the possibilities of rhythm, competing downbeats, waves of repetition and loosely scored playing, as exemplified by Riley's groundbreaking 1964 composition 'In C' (ibid.: 42). What is more, he seized Riley's ideal of a body of individuals with a shared musical purpose and the freedom to uniquely arrive at the goal. After studying in Accra and absorbing Ghanian musical structures, he pursued 'ritualistic activity that subjugated personal expression to communal process' (ibid.:72), transmuting Western forms through such ritual. Rather than imitating African music, he was able to create Western music informed by the values of West African art. In this way, he said, '[O]ne can create a music with one's own sound that is constructed in light of one's knowledge of non-Western structures [. . .]. This brings about the interesting situation of the non-Western influence being there in thinking, but not in sound. [. . . This] is likely to produce something genuinely new' (ibid.).

The Bay Area, with a still-dynamic jazz scene in the early 1970s, provided fertile ground for musical experimentation and hybridization. Like these composers, Molissa was soon able to find a way into a new dance form based on a blending of structures and motifs which led to complex perceptual states that were radical and new, Western as well as non-Western. Louis Horst's ideas of modern and pre-classic dance forms, Laban's effort/shape, Graham's standing leg work, Limon's deep *pliés* and Fuller's rhythmic inspiration were her working tools. Then she applied them to her childhood understanding of performance as a journey 'nested in "life's journey"', where time is progressive and rooted in ongoing individual and cosmic transformation (Drewal 1992: 46). In echo of the myriad celebrations she witnessed and the rituals she spied on as a child, she began to map dances in circles or pulses of motion, so that time unspooled in an unending, overlapping series of visual waves. Like Glass, with whom she would eventually often collaborate, and Reich, she used repetition and polymetre as a foundational strategy. Through rhythms, Molissa could evoke phase patterning that allowed movement to begin in unison, slip unity, create a doubling effect, break apart, then return to unison. Sound phasing causes the ear to hear new sounds from the overlapping audio waves that manifest as echoes and drones; similarly, phase patterning, when applied to bodies, provokes the eye to see ghostly patterns produced by visual neurons that remain active even after the visual stimulus has passed, creating the illusion that the stimulus is ongoing. This illusion is heightened by the stuttering time lag that Molissa creates between one dancer's movements and another's identical but slightly out-of-phase steps, with the result that the mind seems to see bodies in empty space and the blurring of temporal boundaries. As the edges of the past, present and future become frayed, the viewer feels time break away from its neatly quantifiable trajectory and evolve into a constant elastic aliveness, with each element of the space/time triptych of past–present–future penetrating its counterparts.

Not long after Molissa got to New York, she began crafting these seemingly simple basics into a tsunami of postmodern motion, and this, alone, made her noteworthy. But she went further, and infused her dances with ideas of balance, endurance, poise and coolness, creating Western dances with, as Reich said, 'the non-Western influence being there in thinking' (Schwartz: 72). And as she put her distillations on stage, she shook up dance categories and confounded audiences' expectations. She also upset the critics.

Molissa arrived in New York City in 1975, a fearless 21-year-old with a sensuous, chiselled face, a long sinuous torso and single-minded purpose. In 1977, she formed a company, Molissa Fenley and Dancers, and began to make her presence felt with her first pieces, *Planets* and *The Willies*. She then thoroughly woke up New York's downtown scene with the premiere of a 50-minute rhythmic bash called *Mix*—three dancers and herself, moving with maracas, sand blocks and ankle bells, all bodies on deck for the duration of the work, making quick, simple patterns in 4/4 time that grew wild as they moved in counterpoint to their raucous and exuberant clapping and stamping. A work that combined solos, circles and cross patterns, it led to an ingenious and remarkably fresh, open, even joyous celebration that allowed audiences to see in its full glory the growing dishevelment that such prolonged effort brings. Augmented by a miked floor, the dance unfurled like a complex tapestry of sound and motion, the dancers constantly communicating with their eyes subtle movement cues and pleasure-filled gazes at one another. It was a kind of postmodern folk dance of dos-y-dos on steroids, and was reported to have evoked in viewers a sense of both elation and exhaustion. Joy, especially joy combined with gruelling exertion, was not a well-known commodity in the brainy and ultra-cool downtown dance world of 1979. What buoyed and energized this particular joy—what made it and its curious blend of play, virtuosity and ritual seem strange to some audiences—were West African forces redefining the cultural norms of Western performance.

One of the most insightful viewers of Molissa's work at the time was critic and dance scholar Sally Banes who sympathetically called Molissa an outsider in both American and African dance cultures. She also noted that Molissa's work blended 'an African sensitivity to ritual dance, in which music, song, movement, and the symbolism of cultural expression are inextricably woven, with an acute awareness of her heritage as a modernist, American choreographer' (19940: 259). But there Banes stopped. It was a fact that Molissa was not at one with either American or Nigerian dance, that she was never absorbed into black Nigeria. Nevertheless, she experienced herself as a Nigerian girl. And although she was a US citizen with roots in Northern California, she stood at a far remove from the Americans whose childhoods were shaped by the political and cultural tumult of the 1960s, from sit-ins to political assassinations to liberation movements to the counterculture. When it came to her relation to the human form, and the complex role of the body on land, she saw herself as a citizen of the earth, always in motion across its face, schooled in the beauty of Africa and Africans but emboldened by a modern Californian woman's sense of physical and existential freedom. But when it concerned the body per se, her baseline was the disciplined freedoms of the Nigerian form. It was, she said,

> [T]his absolute gorgeous means of transport. This transport doesn't just transport you—it transports everything that we do while carrying a baby, and laughing . . . . I remember once seeing a guy on a bicycle with 10 mattresses on his head . . . [so many] beautiful bodies, beautiful necks and gorgeous strength. That was absolutely exquisite to watch—to be in a world where the body was just so in balance, always in balance. You just couldn't believe it. They carried water on their head and never spilt a drop.[7]

While Banes was attuned to some of the non-Western currents eddying in Molissa's work, quite a few dance writers saw only a whir of rapid-fire, athletic movement, and they interpreted the choreographer's output as a sign of contamination by a raging new cultural phenomenon—the aerobic dance craze and the emergence of jogging as the physical pursuit. Arlene Croce of the *New Yorker* went so far as to assert that the work was more closely allied to American physical culture than to dance, and in one review compared a solo by Molissa to a naked 'sports event'—the kind of dance that is done at half-times and was common on music videos—while dismissing the rest of her choreography as 'regulated material—literally, sports and game': 'She is a bad girl showing off' (2000: 422, 420).

Critic and scholar Lynn Garofalo, confessing in 1985 to disliking Molissa's dance, wrote in the *Berkshire Gazette*: 'Her non-stop aerobics bruised my senses, leaving me by the end of one her marathons like a runner exhausted at the finish line' (1985: n.p.). Advancing this theme to the next step, another critic described Molissa as the 'Fonda of post-modern dance' (Geeslin 1985). One particularly snide pan of three works, by Clive Barnes, describes her work as having 'more in common with calisthenics than dance' (1985: n.p.). Molissa was even compared, sometimes lovingly, other times less so, to the Energizer Bunny, the 1989 Energizer Holdings company mascot that moved in robotic perpetuity.

Clearly, cultural anxiety was in the air. Aerobics was storming the country, covering bodies in brightly coloured high-legged spandex, Jane Fonda its leading doyenne. Joggers in tracksuits with terry-cloth sweatbands were kicking up dust along heavily trafficked roadsides. The man behind this new craze was Dr Kenneth Cooper, a colonel with the US Air Force, assigned to prepare astronauts for space. Later known as 'the father of the modern fitness movement', Cooper began gathering data that proved that aerobic exercise could prevent heart disease and other illnesses associated with affluent, sedentary living. These data were rolled into Cooper's 1968 bestseller *Aerobics*, a book that changed the late-twentieth-century approach to fitness. Then air force nurse, Jackie Sorenson, took inspiration from Cooper and approached him with the idea of a workout routine to music—'dance aerobics', she called it. Cooper urged her on and a woman-centred fitness boom soon swept the country. Although it was easy to ridicule at the time, aerobics was a real threat to dance. Suddenly dance-like workouts that promised toned, sleek bodies in an atmosphere of pop music were siphoning off dance-studio clientele who wanted to experience the joy of moving to music without the pressure of meeting vaulted standards of performance or of joining a priesthood of the arts. Aerobics were cheaper and, besides, the costumes a whole lot sexier.

While Molissa didn't go to aerobics classes, she was introduced to cardiovascular training at Mills, and it would eventually influence her approach to her daily regimen in a fundamental way. As part of a new appreciation for heart–lung health, the Mills Dance Department in the early 1970s brought in kinesiologist Patrice Griffin from the Physical Education Department to work with dancers, since a study had found that dancers, to everyone's surprise, lacked cardiovascular stamina. Molissa already had a life-long love of running—her childhood was filled with swift flight over African bush paths—so she not only took to the new training regimen (it entailed running around the dance building) but also incorporated endurance into her choreography. This became both a mark of her cross-cultural synthesis and an indication of her cheeky willingness to transgress high–low dance boundaries. There was also a deep pragmatism to her inclusion of cardiovascular workouts in her training. Two years after arriving in New York, she jettisoned the historic routine of attending daily dance class, not only because classes were prohibitively expensive but because they were modelled on a passé relationship of choreographer, who functioned as an avatar, and student, whose role was that of an acolyte. Molissa knew that to make a new kind of dance founded on a new paradigm of relations between dancer and dance-maker, she had to find a different way of preparing her instrument. Consequently, like the West Coast iconoclasts before her, she pioneered an idiosyncratic approach to conditioning—hers combined cardiovascular and strength workouts with modern dance technique classes that she administered to herself every day in a dance studio. It is the same that she practises today.

Banes was not alone in seeing that the young dance-maker was on to something new, or in understanding that seeing the work on its own terms demanded new criteria by which to watch. Among the most vocal was Anna Kisselgoff, lead dance critic for the *New York Times*, who seemed to understand most acutely the import of Molissa's physical vibrancy:

> We have seen the dance of the future and it works. In 'Energizer,' a new piece seen Sunday afternoon at the American Theater Laboratory, a very young experimental choreographer named Molissa Fenley creates a tremendously exciting work that blasts her audience into a new, and brave,

> world of dance [. . .]. What is stunning about 'Energizer' is [. . .] its appeal to a kinetic response. [. . .] To concentrate on the formal organization of the piece is to miss its impact (1980: n.p.).

Even in its title, *Energizer* communicates Molissa's intention to fashion a dance as a fierce source of physical power. Kisselgoff underscores this fundamental aspect of Molissa's early dance—the dancer's intense kinetic output creates an equally keen kinesthetic response in the viewer. Other work, like *Hemispheres*, creates a parallel response, and in a quieter way so too do her introspective pieces, such as the homage *Bardo* for visual artist Keith Haring and *In Recognition* for dancer–choreographer Arnie Zane, both of whom died of AIDS, or her *Prop Dances*, all of which are decidedly meditative.

Her first New York City dance *Planets* revealed that she had all the elements of her movement language in place. Beginning with the stripped-down dance action of the legs, she set the lower body loose in rapid rhythmic procession, the engine of time, will, power and endurance, as it is in West African dance (Thompson 1974: 9, 117). Then she forged an iconic counterpoint in the upper body, stretching the torso into torsion and oblique angles, and thrusting the arms in strangely beautiful poses that seemed to float above the lower body as though in another dimension of time (prefiguring by years Merce Cunningham's later computer-generated arm movements). This use of the upper body, rather than being decorative, communicated images and associations that appeared to exist in a time beyond time, reminiscent of the ancient sculpture that inspired her—the Cycladic, Egyptian and Japanese Haniwa. As she evolved this language, she began to make these arms more motional and less static, deepening their mysterious potency. In most of her dances, the dancers share knowing glances as they move through space and create the vectors of the dance. Less consciously, they tie together the gossamer forms—images in the mind's eye—that arise in the intersecting lines as the dance journeys on. This is 'where a sense of inspiration and beauty emerge, disclosing a hidden order'.[8]

In other early dances like *Hemispheres*, Molissa called forth a body that rigorously defied the idea of a female concert dancer as decorous being, someone who had to hide the rigour of her dancing. She openly claimed 'masculine' vigour and endurance and stripped away the illusions of femininity with which women had been required to cloak their ferocious strength and physical prowess as dancers. She also implicitly challenged the idea that visible effort denigrates or threatens the high-minded status of dance, just as the Judson Church pioneers before her challenged the presumption that pedestrian movement—vernacular language of the body—could never be rendered art. Not only did Molissa not hide her effort, she also presented it with stunning, self-assured and unabashed West African 'mystic coolness' (Thompson 1983: 16), claiming the right to be visibly strong. She used drive, energy and endurance to prove that women could express nearly mythic physical capacity with unapologetic elan. In doing so, she upended the genteel boundaries of performance and joyously reformulated late twentieth-century dance with new notions of ritual, effort and identity. Some critics scoffed and grew restive; Molissa became a Soho pop star.

If the artistic community had little difficulty grasping that Molissa was pushing herself and her dancers to their physical edge as part of a goal far grander than anything mere 'regulated material' could achieve, what was less obvious was its kinship with Yoruban moral and aesthetic virtues of balance, grace and endurance. In the Yoruban world view, balance is the measure of one's existential rightness with an indeterminate and always transforming cosmic whole (Omófolábo 1998: 36). The source and conduit of this balance is the body/mind, our states of being manifested through posture, gait and facial expressions (Thompson 1974: 96). When we are able to withstand a whirlwind of opposing forces in the cosmos, we have achieved a supple mind, or 'inner head', and such suppleness leads to poised, multilayered interaction. Such spritely engagement, in turn, endows physical form with beauty, lucidity and rigour, and such expression of life force then reciprocally reinforces the state of interior equipoise.

For a performer, the ultimate test of her moral and aesthetic equilibrium is to maintain inner balance during extreme physical challenge and exertion; onlookers see only external grace, even radiance, not duress (Omófolábo 1998: 29–30).

Echoing Yoruban dance spectacles, Molissa created choreographic physical challenges as concurrent spiritual trials. In her hands, the dance body was not a mere metaphor for the metaphysical body—the body qua body was itself beautiful and worthy of admiration because it overlapped the metaphysical body, as the life/world and the otherworld overlap for the Yoruba, sharing a place and time where interpenetration of these realms is possible. By relying on phase patterning and polymetre to carry her spare Western dance forms, and making works that were tests of endurance, she gave her audiences a glimpse into the otherworld that she believed the body implicitly and often unknowingly inhabits. Part of her brilliance was her ability to utilize the complex values of West Africa and place them in concert with late-twentieth-century athleticism to mould an Olympian female body charged with what, at times, has been shamanistic potency.

Nowhere is that daring more evident than in her tour de force, *State of Darkness*. This solo, made for herself, was set to Igor Stravinsky's 33-minute *Rite of Spring*, written between 1912 and 1913 for Ballets Russes' wunderkind Vaslav Nijinsky. The score, which remains a throbbing and beautifully cacophonous piece of music, was written for Nijinsky's 'primitivist' ballet and ignited a brawl at the Champs-Elysees Theatre in Paris in 1913. While no fights broke out when Molissa took the stage, certain quarters of the dance world again looked askance at her. This time she had the audacity to shift from ensemble to solo work, and her plan to dance alone to Stravinsky's score was viewed as either suicide or sheerest arrogance. She was unflappable—each day she felt Stravinsky, Nijinsky and Mikhail Baryshnikov watch over her daunting efforts in the now-defunct downtown studio of the Dia Foundation. There she made her phrases in a fog of pale light, the visible and invisible worlds keeping her company as she built the dance phrase by phrase, arc by arc. The premiere was her incendiary declaration of independence.

Commissioned by the American Dance Festival, the dance opened at the Reynolds Theater at Duke University in 1988, launching her new solo career. She went for broke. Dancing alone on stage for the full 33 minutes, she enacted a ritual ordeal of birth, death and rebirth. Her lean androgynous form was dressed only in black tights, her rib cage at times fluttering bird-like with the rapid bellow action of her lungs, her only companion being David Moodey's haunting atmosphere of light and dark and the cacophonous score. It was perhaps her most difficult trial of all, and in it she met each challenge like Psyche before the impossible tasks set by Aphrodite. Molissa shapeshifted from masculine to feminine, from human to animal, from quotidian to mythic. Using energy and duration as her tools, she danced with a relentless fervency until she stepped into the light at the end. As Omófolábo Àjàyí writes, '[I]t is the height of virtuosity for a dancer, even after a long spell of exhaustive dancing, to emerge *immediately after* totally composed yet exuding intense vitality and alertness, the sweating and panting breath the only telltale sign of the physical exertion recently experienced' (1998: 32). In meeting this standard of virtuosity, Molissa invited audiences to become witness to an ancient-seeming yet deeply modernist ritual that offered a noble and daring vision of female liberation in place of the historic vision of female sacrifice.

If *State of Darkness* was a manifesto about the new female body and, by extension, about the reclamation of female power from a mythology of female sacrifice embedded in the culture, her body boldly proclaimed what was required: extreme discipline and effort, unflagging grace in the face of trials and unyielding fearlessness. As with her prior body of work, it drew upon repetition in sync and out, the mythic demarcation of space and the iconic use of limbs interspersed with minute flutterings reminiscent of bird wings and skittering insects. She also presented a vision of freedom from the reductive binaries of gender (even of species) and the Cartesian divide between matter and mind. While the phenomenal world dominated, out of it arose intimations of the metaphysical, inviting the audience to join Molissa in both the life/world of mundane existence and the otherworld of forces beyond our ken, using incantatory waves of rhythmically complex phrases crafted from extreme bodily exertion. The aim was a liminal space that opened the door to *communitas*—the shared yet unique participation by all present (Turner 2008: 127). Moodey's beautiful pools of light and shade helped make that possible.

Although *State of Darkness* may be the most celebrated and incendiary dance of her career, Molissa continues to create work of subtle ceremonial depth and sublime concentration. In 2010, she completed a round of prop dances, each dance wedded to an object or set of objects that become extensions of the body. One of the works, *Mass Balance*, involves the choreographer–dancer balancing a 10-foot, 5- to 10-pound pole at an elegant geologic pace. It is an homage to and study of the tipping point of Arctic ice, as the balance between the melting ice and its accumulation is disturbed, a formalist study of physical exertion and extreme mental concentration, and a prayer and a lament for the natural world. This kind of humanist, physically vigorous approach to abstraction has informed Molissa's methods from the outset.

For over three decades, Molissa has transmitted life force in highly patterned, repetitive, enigmatic and evocative forms, inviting viewers into an almost-pulsating relationship. When we accept the invitation, our bodies join in a kinaesthetic field of action and perception, and we meet in the in-between or transitional space where intimate relationships get shaped and creativity unleashed (see Winnicott 1953). In this transitional space, she helps blossom a series of overlapping worlds that are at once archaic, modern, postmodern, non-Western and decidedly Western.

Walking by the river that day in July made me want to wrestle with Molissa's relationship with space, time and energy, in and out of the theatre. I came to understand that whether it's the Joyce or a crowded city street, space for her is an arena of sleeping potential. Throughout her illustrious career, she has worked hard to awaken that potential. She merged the freedoms she found in Nigeria with the forms she learnt in California; in New York, she made dances with the body as both a divining and a lightning rod, a messenger that alerts us to the mystery and power of the complex journey we are on. In the process, she has revolutionized our concept of what it is to dance.

Notes

1 Molissa Fenley, interview with the author, New York Library for the Performing Arts, 28 June 2010.

2 Ibid.

3 Ibid.

4 Ibid.

5 Molissa Fenley, interview with the author, Oakland, California, March 2011.

6 Rebecca Fuller, interview with the author, Sebastapol, California, 30 April 2010.

7 Fenley, interview with the author, 2010.

8 See Molissa Fenley's essay in this volume, pp. 61.

Works Cited

ÀJÀYÍ, Omófolábo. 1998. *Yoruba Dance: The Semiotics of Movement and Body Attitude in Nigerian Culture.* Trenton: African Press West.

BANES, Sally. 1980. '"Drive," She Said: The Dance of Molissa Fenley' in *Writing Dancing in the Age of Postmdernism.* Hanover: Wesleyan University Press, pp. 259–68.

BARNES, Clive. 1985. 'Step & Turn & Call it Modern'. *New York Post,* 21 November, n.p.

CROCE, Arlene. 2000. *Writing in the Dark: Dancing in the 'New Yorker'.* New York: Farrar, Straus and Giroux.

DREWAL, Margaret Thompson. 1992. *Yoruba Ritual: Performers, Play, Agency.* Bloomington: Indiana University Press.

DYER, Geoff. 1997. *Out of Sheer Rage: Wrestling with D. H. Lawrence.* New York: North Point Press.

GAROFALO, Lynn. 1985. 'Molissa Fenley at Pillow'. *The Berkshire Eagle*, 7 August, n.p.

GEESLIN, Neal. 1985. 'Riding the Radical Next Wave, Super-fit Molissa Fenley is the Fonda of Post-modern Dance'. *People* 24(25) (16 December): n.p.

KISSELGOFF, Anna. 1980. 'Dance: Molissa Fenley's "Energizer"'. *New York Times*, 11 November, n.p.

SCHWARTZ, K. Robert. 1996. *Minimalists*. London: Phaidon.

THOMPSON, Robert Farris. 1974. *African Art in Motion: Icon and Act*. Berkeley: University of California Press.

——. 1983. *Flash of the Spirit: African and Afro-American Art and Philosophy*. New York: Random House.

TURNER, Victor. 2008. *The Ritual Process: Structure and Anti-structure*. Piscataway: Transaction Publishers.

WINNICOTT, D. W. 1953. 'Transitional Objects and Transitional Phenomena'. *The International Journal of Psychoanalysis* 34: 89–97.

IMAGE 9 *Sightings* (1993); in performance at the Joyce Theater, New York; set by Tatsuo Miyajima. Photograph by Tom Brazil © 1993.

An Interview with Peter Boal

Ann Murphy

Peter Boal, current artistic direct of Pacific Northwest Ballet in Seattle, was a premier danseur at New York City Ballet from 1983 to 2005, beloved for his elegant classicism and unswerving humility. Unlike many of his classical dance peers, Boal attended an array of dance events outside the arena of Lincoln Center, where New York City Ballet continues to be in residence. He itched to take on new challenges, so when he was urged to see Molissa Fenley, he went. This interview was conducted by phone by Ann Murphy in October 2009.

What led you to look for other work to perform?

From day one, I wanted to keep extending myself in different directions, so that meant asking for roles at New York City Ballet that I wouldn't have been considered for. I was initially perceived as a purely classical ballet dancer, and I wanted to demonstrate that I could be more than just that, that I could dance more contemporary work or pieces that involved more acting. I was always looking for that next challenge. I liked to say that I was artistically restless. You conquer one thing, then you want the next, harder, thing.

My friend Jeff Edwards had seen Molissa perform in Asia. He said 'You must see this woman when she comes to New York.' He took me to the Joyce. I had heard of Molissa but hadn't seen her dance. She was doing *State of Darkness*, and that was my introduction to the world of Molissa Fenley. The irony is that some of my purity and classicism came through in my performances of Molissa's work. You can't get far away from it when it is who you are.

Had you been going to downtown dance at that point? What was going on that made you look outside the ballet for work?

I was going to the Joyce regularly, whether it was for Elliot Feld, Jennifer Muller or Elisa Monte. I was sampling here and there. Someone would have an extra ticket. Or I wanted to see Pilobolus. I made it as far as City Center. I had done some work with Wendy Perron. She'd created a solo for me. She was the first person connected with a dance scene different from what I'd known.

Did some of your colleagues venture out also? Was this something you did in off times or was it percolating continuously?

When there was a lay-off, my colleagues got into a group to do the same repertory we'd been doing all year, then take it on the road. I don't think people were really looking to extend themselves into the world of the modern dancer, although [Mikhail] Baryshnikov was. Even though he wasn't a colleague of mine, he was looking for a different direction and that had an impact. Twyla [Tharp] had been downtown dance and he brought her into the mainstream. Whether or not you like him, he affects everybody in ballet.

I was also very affected by Nederlands Dans 3, a company for dancers over 40. They danced some of the most artistically powerful dance I've ever seen. They were classical ballet dancers looking beyond, to see what else they could do. Whenever Nacho Duato's company came to town, I'd see them.

Do you feel that this was intellectually driven, or did this have to do with ageing as a dancer?

I don't think I was ageing yet, although by the time I started working with Molissa regularly, I was in the second half of my career—the twilight years. But initially it was just a cool choice, and interesting.

Were you an athlete as a kid?

Yeah, track and field.

And how did you get to the city from your parents' home in Bedford?

Ultimately on the train, but initially my parents had to hire a driver because it was a long way to go—about an hour or so. The ballet schools in Westchester didn't have any boys in their classes, so that pushed me to the School of American Ballet, which was good.

Had you ever seen Joffrey's Rite of Spring?

No.

And before you set out to do Molissa's piece, did you look at The Rite of Spring?

No, I looked at Molissa.

Tell me about the experience of going to see Molissa.

I was blown away. I remember being struck by how there were some of the same concepts that I'd grown to love in [George] Balanchine's work—a purity of movement and line, an elimination of excess, no elaborate costumes, no elaborate sets. It was just pared down to choreography, music and movement. I also thought Molissa's body worked in such a logical way. It really had a connection to classical ballet. It wasn't that I thought, 'Oh, she works like a ballet dancer,' but there was something in her ideals that seemed familiar to me.

Can you elaborate on the logic in how she worked? What in the movement seemed logical to you?

There was no struggle and there was great focus. There was such technique in the work, which is what classical ballet is all built on. You can layer the technique with emotion as you get good at it but, really, you have to find the balances, you have to establish the lines, you have to demonstrate the control. Molissa was doing all of that. It was slightly different from ballet, of course, with the standing leg in a bent rather than elongated position. There wasn't the same effort to get away from the floor that ballet dancers are known for—she had more of a relationship with the floor. Still, the beauty of her arm movements and the angles of her neck seemed to come from the same camp that I'd grown up in.

And seeing the work, what did you understand it to be?

I was so impressed with this one single individual. Maybe that she was a woman was partly why I was so impressed. The fact that she did three solos in one night—at so many levels, I couldn't believe it. There was this confidence in herself, this belief in her craft. I wasn't alone—that's how the audience's responsded too. I was stunned. But I was curious too, to know whether it was the power of the choreography or the power of the performer that hit me. You couldn't separate them when you saw her do a one-woman show. Did you stand up to applaud the physical aspect of the performer? Or did you stand up to applaud the choreographic contribution? That's what fascinated me later, because, by working together, we were obviously going to separate that.

Did you come to a decision about that later?

I did, because we put another performer into her choreography and got incredible results. So it was a testament to phenomenal choreography. But I still didn't know if we were standing on our feet and giving an ovation to choreographic content or to the performer's ability to 'kill it'.

That takes me back to what you saw and experienced in the choreography. Did the movement, in a sense, transcend itself as you learnt and performed it?

I found the movement fascinating. The way Molissa worked was not to tell me what the movement was and watch me do it, but to consistently do it next to me. Lke two people jumping out of a plane together—you have to do it as bodies plummeting in order to do it the first time. It was a hand-holding process, like teaching a child to ride a bike . . . like when, eventually the parents stop holding the back of the bike and the child goes off on his own. It felt like that.

Would she stand next to you or in front of you?

Her choreography turns around so much that it kept changing. I suppose it would start with her 6 feet to the right and 2 feet downstage so I could get her out of the corner of my eye. I wouldn't really watch her much—I would more sense and feel her. The funny thing was that she admitted after about three weeks of dancing side by side that she couldn't see anything without her glasses! She thought the blob next to her was doing the right thing but she wasn't sure. And then it was just as important and wonderful when she sat on the floor and watched it—that's when she let go of the bike.

It was really a transmission process.

I would say: Is that a pirouette? And she would say: 'It's a turn.' I would say: 'Is it an *arabesque*?' And she would say: 'It's a leg extension to the back.' She actually speaks the ballet vocabulary quite well. I would for my process have to call it a *pas de bourre* while for her it would be a step-ball-change. There was a lot of terminology we would exchange—we educated each other along the way.

What I was fascinated by in Ellen Bromberg's documentary was how you took the ballet out of the steps. I watched you translate the dance into ballet terminology and then erase some of that classicism.

In translating into ballet, I was using my memory game to remember what was next, and then I would try to erase it. I was trying to be Molissa Fenley 100 per cent. I failed, but I failed successfully.

Can you dive into that a little bit? What was the process of becoming Molissa Fenley 100 per cent?

I always felt like clay as a dancer. Whatever exact angle Jerome Robbins wanted the head at, I wanted to do that angle. I didn't want to put my own stamp on it. I was trying to get the vocabulary down perfectly and would look very closely at videotapes. Molissa was the one who sometimes pushed me away from that. She'd say, 'I wish you would do this mistake that you make because I actually like it better than what I did.' She thought I should do it in a more balletic direction in places, or if I was going to add an extra turn—because we work on those pirouettes so often in ballet—to put the extra turn in even though she hadn't. So she was encouraging me to find some of my own voice in the piece, even as far as the nature of the steps.

To back up for a moment: Did you have a narrative take of the whole piece or did you see it as a series of moments and movements?

Molissa would feed me some narrative, but she didn't overdo or overtalk it. She would say, simply, that she was guarding against a spirit that was downstage at this moment. Then remind me that 'When you're in the crouching position, facing in the same direction, the theme will come in in five minutes.' She made me aware of certain ghosts, certain references, particularly by the names of the sections. There's one section called 'Organic Farming' where you distribute seeds into the earth. There's a reference to the ground and a reference to the sky. They're light—they're abstract references—but they're helpful for the performer as a reference, because it makes you come from the place she intends. It probably gives that very light reference to the audience, though it can take what it wants from it. All the same, it helps to have some kind of guide in a performer's mind.

How did you translate for yourself that State of Darkness *is, in essence, a fertility rite?*

She would mention it, but in her process it became different things. For me, it was as much a fertility rite as it was Molissa staking a claim to a piece of the world of dance. The sense of history that comes to you through the music is overwhelming. You can't escape it. One can easily picture the choreography for *Rite* as having at least 40 dancers, maybe even some animals, whereas she allowed the music to be the community and she the protagonist.

IMAGE 10, (facing page) IMAGE 11 *Esperanto* (1985); Molissa Fenley, Jill Diamond, Scottie Mirvis in photo session, New York; costumes by Jean-Paul Gaultier. Photograph by Chris Callis © 1985.

Did you study the music at all before embarking?

No, no. I just listened to it endlessly, unless that means studying . . .

Were you familiar with the sections as Stravinsky named them, or did you leave that alone?

No, I was not familiar with them, unless Molissa told me, and I don't think she did.

Did you play with gender in the dance? Molissa can visibly do it because she's topless and has breasts. Was there any kind of parallel gender play for you?

No. There were a few steps that were overtly feminine steps. I just did them as they were given, but they didn't read feminine on me. There were places where the waist would really twist at the same time as the wrists would really bend, and the elbows, and there was sort of an alluring strut. These were much more feminine moments than others, and I had to take them on wholeheartedly, so I don't know if they were read as feminine or if they were read as twisted contortions which I moved through. I was trying to imitate Molissa, and Molissa has this amazing masculine power for all her petite feminine form. If anything, the masculinity suited the piece, and, of course, I went with that.

Can you talk about the micro-movements in the work and what your relationship to those were?

Those were hard for me because they were little tiny jitters of the head, and I hadn't been that fine-tuned in classical ballet. Hand movements? Basically there's one hand that you want to achieve. It can breathe slightly but with Molissa there were really very specific hand movements that became weapons and shields and defensive hand positions ready for offence. I had to really study those. In the past, I had studied choreography for legs, arms, but hands I hadn't thought about as much. It made me a better ballet dancer to think like that.

Because it made you more flexible as a ballet dancer?

It made me think down through the tip of the digits. We certainly think about toes a lot, and actually I had to think less about toes—

there were places when I didn't want to cup the foot because it wasn't something that Molissa did, so I tried to keep my foot more pedestrian. The arm movements were always very particular. She really delves into specific torso movements as well, and sometimes only the left side of the rib cage is leading a movement. There is more symmetry and balance in classical ballet, and here I was working more with asymmetry.

You've clearly danced to Stravinsky before, but did you find Molissa's metres notable or difficult?

Stravinsky actually helped me, because the music was familiar. I'd presented five other pieces of dance to Stravinsky before, so it was a bit like that familiar suit you put on. The variation of the music was also so tremendous that your mind went into the section you were in through listening to the music. That was a plus for me. Such familiarity helped.

How Molissa marks the stage seems more archetypical than most ballet usage of the stage. Were the stage landmarks absorbed by you physically or did you have place names for them like when you go into the shadow or come into the light?

I've always thought very geometrically as a dancer—we work so much with quarter marks, centre marks, eighth marks, third wing, fourth wing. That's one thing I can do well—get a sense of how many steps I would need to hit a mark and how big those steps would have to be. It helps me process a piece to know how I'm going to do it spatially.

One of the things I loved about Molissa's choreography was that there were zones—power centres—around the stage and I would go into them. Mentally, you can flip out in a solo that's 33 minutes long, so you need anchors and familiarity and things to think about to get through it.

Let's talk about that. How did you mentally approach the 33 minutes?

First, I won't let a challenge take me down and I saw that about Molissa. She said it was humanly possible, and I figured if Molissa

Fenley can do it, I'm going to do it too. When I did my first night alone, I did a solo recital with three solos. I never would have tried it if I hadn't known that Molissa did it regularly for years. I was up for the challenge and it was the greatest challenge I ever faced. The premiere was especially brutal, because it was 80 degrees and one of those hot August nights in New York City, the humidity off the charts. It was hard and I thought I was going to go down there.

What kept your mind focused in the 33 minutes?

It's really as much a mind game as it is a physical one. There are parts that I really relished, and I'd know they were coming and look forward to them. Then there's a very long, quiet section that comes in the middle where you can actually let your mind focus less and go into the zone. That's kind of nice. In every piece I've danced, I believed there was a centre and I'd find it. There was about a four-count moment in *State* that, for me, was the centre—when I'm standing centrestage, looking out beyond the audience, palms facing the audience, my legs in a very comfortable position and suddenly I begin to sway. It was the most minimal movement in the entire 33 minutes. I saw that the dance worked its way down to that movement and then worked its way back up and out.

I also think of dances geometrically—usually in halves, sometimes in thirds. It's a little like counting to 25. You can think: 'Well, it's in groups of 5,' or 'I'd like to split it somewhere between 12 and 13.' There were times when I could be lost in the piece, think less and just enjoy the spontaneity of it; there were times when I had to completely focus, whether it was on counting or listening to the music or remembering the words that Molissa had given me.

How did you regard that lighting in the piece?

That's another thing—the lighting helped—a bit like Stravinsky. I think the lighting is important for the choreography as wonderful as it is. To ask an audience to watch one body for a long period of time is a challenge. In the ballets I know, the longest anyone is on stage alone is about three minutes and then a corps de ballet comes out, then there's a *pas de deux*, then there's the all-girls dance. The constantly rotating palette of light helped audiences. For lack of better words, you saw the dancer in a different light every few minutes. In a way, you could see a different individual each time.

Did you feel at all like the lighting was your partner?

You certainly felt with Dave Moodey's designs that there was another artist on stage with you enhancing your performance, just like Stravinsky. It made a big difference.

Did you wear black tights?

We experimented a little bit. I started out a little darker than flesh-coloured tights. Molissa wanted to try that—a bit more an image of the new-born finding its way in the wild forests. Ultimately she liked the classic look—it's almost Balanchinian with those black tights—so we went back to the black tights, and, of course, the bare chest.

How many times did you perform it?

I think five or six, it wasn't that many.

All in New York?

No, I did the first one in Damrosch Park—that was the hot one. Then I did two at the Kitchen. Then two in Salt Lake City at the University of Utah, with Molissa there. There were five in all.

Molissa talked about creating the piece in the Dia Center studio and that she imagined Nijinsky, Diaghilev and Baryshnikov hovering in the corners. Did you have any ghosts that guided you as you learnt it or performed it?

I guess Balanchine is always a ghost in my life, mostly because I knew him a little bit and I've lived in his work my whole life. I still do. I almost always think of him before I go on stage. No matter what I'm dancing. I'm not a religious person but it's almost like I ask for his blessing—I hate to use the word blessing—or his approval. I think of him and it seems the right thing to do. Some people are crossing themselves or doing other things. I think of Balanchine before I go on stage. I didn't have the mental connections with Diaghilev or Nijinsky. Baryshnikov did come in to watch us rehearse, which was great, and gave me some valuable advice on performing. How to approach the stamina aspects of it and to make sure I didn't do 100 per cent the whole time because then you can't appreciate 100 per cent. You have to turn in something a little quieter at times so that the bigger moments seem big. I always had Molissa not as a ghost but as a vital human presence standing right there in the wings, enjoying the performance, helping with the performance and pulling for me.

Can you describe more what you derived from the experience of working with her?

I loved it. I loved that Dia Center. It was like a meditation session. I love to work. I love to dance completely, full out. This was very different. It's hard to stay with one job for 22 years—it was an amazing job dancing with New York City Ballet all those years but I tended to really relish the work outside the company as well. For me, the last 9 years with teaching was very important and working with Molissa covered those last 10 years of my career. It was another thing that I could enjoy, and I think it made it easier knowing that I had this artistic fulfilment to accompany that one.

Do you feel that it changed you at all as an artist? Did it influence what you did with your own company?

I think Molissa's choreography is an education in how an audience will see work, because you can draw an audience into the tiniest detail but you have to do it effectively or they'll lose interest. As she is so focused in all of her performances, she asks the same of her audience. Her choreography was instructive in how I could do that. So that was beneficial when I went back to ballet. I knew I would think: 'Even if the stage is full of dancers and sets, where is their eye now? Whereas I might have done a bigger gesture to capture their attention, I'm going to now experiment with how small and subtle I can do that.' I really got that through working with Molissa.

Did working with her push you in any way to see what else is out there?

She was doing her one-woman show all over the globe. She did it quite often at the Joyce. So when I was looking to start Peter Boal's Solos, the first thing I did in 2003 was that I went to the Joyce. I used Dave Moodey. I asked Molissa to choreograph a piece, so I had three choreographers do three solos. I used Molissa's manager. I used her for advice. I used her foundation for my charitable giving. So it was really under the umbrella of her organization, and by borrowing a lot of her concepts.

Do you find your experience not just with Molissa but with Perron and other postmodern choreographers has affected your approach to ballet?

Oh I think so. To bring Molissa's work to the ballet stage—I don't know if anyone's done that. It was so rewarding for me as a performer and as an artist, and I wanted to give it to some of these artists here at Pacific Northwest Ballet [PNB]. I also wanted to give it to the audience, because I don't think a classical ballet audience would have gone to see or know Molissa Fenley, and I knew she needed a bigger audience. I actually got a lot of rewards out of the fact that a huge portion of the New York City Ballet audience came down to the Joyce where they may not've been before, that they heard about this choreographer Molissa Fenley whom they should have known, that they followed me and they found her. So that was good for both of us. And of course we've done work here by Susan Marshall and Trisha Brown—you don't find their work in classical ballet companies either. There's something very exciting about classical ballet dancers doing work that wasn't created by classical ballet choreographers. These are artists who have discovered themselves and then rediscovered themselves with choreographers outside their familiar territory.

Did all three of your chosen dancers at PNB perform State of Darkness?

Yes. In 2007.

I remember hearing about Molissa's injury [1995], because the dance world heard about it. Whether or not you were in ballet, it was a news item. I think it's interesting that borne of that tragedy . . .

[At that time, though, we] had never met. I ran into her at the opening of a Matisse exhibit at the Museum of Modern Art. I walked up to her and I said: 'You're Molissa Fenley, aren't you? I'm a fan of yours.' And she said: 'You're Peter Boal, and I'm a fan of yours.' She'd been in the City Ballet audience and I'd been in her audience. Then she started stalking me a little bit—I started getting postcards from Hawaii saying 'Maybe you'd like to come by and watch rehearsal,' which I did one day and I just loved—it was at the Dia Center. She didn't want to go on stage and present a solo show for a week again without covers—alternates—because it had been a disaster when she was injured. She couldn't refund all those tickets. Obviously, if she couldn't dance, the show was sunk. So she had alternates. It was such a great artistic decision but it was borne of a necessity that wasn't artistic. That terrible injury was a mixed blessing. While it was so wonderful that she would go into the studio every day and make this work and then present it, it was also wonderful when she went into the studio with me, went into the studio with all these other dancers here at PNB and in New York.

I think it shattered the myth that some people may have had that this was idiosyncratic work that really only Molissa could do.

It might well have been lost if only she had done it. This way it has the potential to live on for ever with other artists presenting it.

IMAGE 12 *Geologic Moments* (1986); Silvia Martins, Molissa Fenley, Christopher Mattox in performance at the Brooklyn Academy of Music, New York. Photograph by Martha Swope © 1986.

IMAGE 13 *Geologic Moments* (1986); Scottie Mirviss, Molissa Fenley, Silvia Martins in performance at the Brooklyn Academy of Music, New York. Photograph by Martha Swope © 1986.

Intuition and Magic

Molissa Fenley

The studio I'm in is immense, silent, calm. All its windows are frosted; light gets in but no details. There's a skylight overhead and Dan Flavin's sconces are on the walls, though rarely turned on. Along one side is a wall of mirrors; there's Laura Dean's marley laid on the floor and a boom box in the corner. Otherwise the studio is open space filled with my accumulated thoughts from my early career, when I worked here regularly. Two people provided this refuge—Joan Duddy and Charles Wright, who occupied offices downstairs. They understood that a consistent space to work in is essential for an artist. In 1986, when I asked Joan how long I could continue to rehearse upstairs, she said, 'Well, how long are you going to be dancing?' Charlie, meanwhile, believed that space = thinking = creativity = artistic results.

For more than 10 years, I was in this studio almost every day. Each session seemed timeless, and my dance experiments were like daydreams. Pieces seemed to make themselves on their own, and I watched the process as it moved me along. This was a time when I was between places to live, when photographer Sandi Fellman said I could live in her photography studio—I had to be out by 10 a.m., home after 6 p.m. My life was simple: I stayed away all day, made work, then came back at night and thought about what I had created.

Now it is the summer of 2010 and I am here in the immense studio again, after being away for 14 years, merged with part of my artistic past. And now the Joyce Soho owns the studio—bought from the Dia Arts Foundation—and Joan and Charles have moved on. This time I am here with the aim of reconstructing my three-part work *Regions* under the auspices of the National Endowment for the Arts' American Masterpieces initiative. Now that I am working in the studio again, my memories of the space have been awakened. These memories lead me to wonder how my past affects the works I make.

Intuition

I think back to when I was a young girl, growing up in Ibadan, Nigeria. I saw an enormous amount of Yoruban dance—dance that took place at all times of the day and night, dance made in celebration of the passages of human life, for puberty or marriage, for birth or for death. I experienced the dances with young eyes, immeasurably excited and engaged, watching everything, taking everything in, storing it for the future. I knew from an early age that there was something about this extreme understanding of the rhythmic passage of time that was going to be a major part of my life. I felt connected to it; dance and rhythm were fundamental to me. Whether the dances were of a religious nature or celebratory, I knew they were necessary and symbolic. And they gave me a radical initiation into the idea of dance as a monumental and essential part of one's life.

When I started making dances after moving to New York, I searched for a personal movement vocabulary that could express a similar force of the monumental, the necessary. I looked for inspirations and one of the first came from Egyptian hieroglyphics—their two-dimensional, flat, planar forms became my starting point. To find movement, I would walk around the studio with my arms angled at 90 degrees, like an Egyptian figure. I started two-dimensionally, added the torque of the torso, and suddenly curves, planes and spirals appeared. As I wondered how to move this torqued torso through space, I looked for a rhythmic baseline in the lower body and added the torqued, angled upper body as melody.

From Egyptian drawings, I moved into ancient sculptures of the human body; those gave me a lot to think about, especially in terms of gesture. Regardless of the period of the sculpture, I could see that gesture was the one thing that connected my body with the human body across time. I discovered that Cycladic sculpture, from the early Bronze Age (around 2600 BCE), has an especially beautiful means of revealing the body by a process of abstraction, where human form is rendered through the elegant clarity of essential lines and the body portrayed as a spare, geometric ideal of balance and proportion, with the arms often held in horizontal or diagonal lines across the torso. Echoing Cycladic gesture in my work became a way for me to connect my contemporary body with the ancient ones.

Another form of ancient sculpture which I found inspiring was the terracotta Haniwa, placed on funerary mounds in Japan during the Yayoi period (300 BCE–300 CE). Like Cycladic forms, the Haniwa figurines possess an abstract beauty that speaks to the elegance and spiritual potential of the human body. Their forms are rendered through a few exacting strokes to suggest arms, shoulders, torso, chin. And they stand in protective and salutary stance, bridges between the living and the dead. I have also absorbed the soft flow of the arms and hands in hula, the rhythmic variety of the arms in Yoruba dance and the arms' exploration of unseen space behind the body in flamenco. In each case, I find gesture to be the most communicative aspect of the body across time. By abstracting gesture in my choreography, I leave it wide open, free of reference to any one culture. It expresses something fundamental about the human form, and underscores the importance of the upper body, face and hands in the acts of understanding, identification and empathic connection.

Another source of inspiration were my travels to Japan where I came in contact with Noh. In Noh, one step can represent many years and a figure on stage can exist between worlds or times—future or past. Travel through space is therefore symbolic and multi-dimensional, not linear; and in order to impart this depth, each performed moment has to be filled with utmost commitment and surety. As scholar Ernest Fenollosa writes, 'The beauty and power of Noh lie in the concentration. The emotion is always fixed upon idea, not upon personality' (Fenollosa and Pound 1916: 120).

There is also widespread use of allusion in Noh—no explicit suggestion, only indirect references to ideas or images. Consequently, no one moment is ever too direct or singular in its meaning. It is an approach that always allows for many points of view and imaginative directions. I have been inspired by its belief in beauty, elegance, refinement and abstraction, by this art that concentrates more on essence than on direct imitation of life.

Tapping into these influences and sources is a daily occurrence. It comes easily and, now that I'm choreographing a new dance, it is effortless. Knowing and intuition take over. Movement arrives without forethought. The dance seems to make itself and, as it does, the body follows pattern which evolves into a recurring system. Periodicity arises and cycles appear. The structure and meaning of the dance reveal themselves.

In my solo choreography, I formally work with the idea of the individual in space, the space changed by the individual's presence and the presence of the individual altered by her placement in space. In my ensemble work, I am concerned with the space around the dancers and the group's intersections and weavings. I like to have the perception of space shift as the movement travels from one dancer to the next. Through counterpoint or resonant repetition, for instance, I might make one dancer's spatial patterns echo another's to create a subliminal after-image. I choose movement that refers back to the source even as it continuously evolves.

IMAGE 14 *Separate Voices* (1987); Molissa Fenley in photo session in New York; costume by Sandi Fellman. Photograph by Sandi Fellman © 1987.

IMAGE 15 *Separate Voices* (1987); Molissa Fenley in photo session in New York; costume by Sandi Fellman. Photograph by Sandi Fellman © 1987.

Space is also defined by rhythm and I organize the choreography's rhythmic layers in parallel frames of time. Sometimes, each dancer moves in her own rhythmic trajectory. Sometimes, all the dancers' rhythms are eclectically layered in unison. Other times, I might inject an element of asymmetrical phrasing and syncopation and juxtapose it to an opposite dynamic. Another level of nuance is created by the individuality of the dancer which brings a particular voice to the translation of the dance.

I also think of space in terms of volume. I envision a dancer's space as inside/outside another's—for instance, a square inside a circle, a circle inside a triangle, a triangle inside a square. In thinking about space, one also has to face the shared space of doer and watcher—doer on the stage, watcher in the audience; doer in the light, watcher in the darkness. These become shared spaces: the mental space of the performer, the space among dancers, the space separating the dancers and the audience, or the clear space around the solo dancer in the volume of the stage where the height, width and depth of the stage uniquely create and communicate meaning. Dancers and audience all share a back wall, although they are reversed—the audience looks to the stage and the wall behind the dancer, while the dancer looks out to the audience and the wall behind it. The result—we are all held in the same rectangular box. The theatre's enclosed space encloses everyone.

Magic

Magic uncovers instinct and innate impulse. It produces qualities of awe, wonder and strangeness, and intuition gives us access to it. By taking instruction from my intuition as I make work, magic arises from dance's pure forms of shape and line, light and shadow. Dancing becomes elemental, forceful, direct and vital.

Witches' Float, created in collaboration with artist Kiki Smith, emerged from an idea of strangeness, where the contemporary body is thrust into an enigmatic place. The stage space is a haunted world that alludes to magic and ritual—particularly to the Salem witch trials of 1692 and its judges who decreed that, to uncover witches, suspected women were to be tied to chairs and thrown in the river. If one floated, a witch she was. Of course, not one floated.

The piece incorporates three unearthly and untouchable sculptures by Kiki. The first is of a floating woman, whose luminousness reveals her to be a source of power and influence. The dancer dances beneath the levitated sculpture as well as in the area that extends before it, animating the space with the floater's power. The next is a cocoon shaped as a trace of a woman with generic rather than individual features. The dancer's role is that of an emissary who gathers forces from the floating figure and relays them to the nascent figure—she is animated through her interaction with the floater and, embodying the strangeness of the cocoon figure, she then continues to the third sculpture. The third sculpture is the Witness—she has been in darkness throughout the work, watching time unfold. The dancer is between the states of discovery and action and now has to do as the Witness requires. The Witness has messages only the dancer can hear; once she has imparted them, the dancer returns to the floater with that new knowledge, her trials accomplished, the cycle completed.

The dancer's body is painted red. She is of no specific gender and from no single culture. The bright red flesh of her chest and back and her skin looks flayed; we are all red under our skin.

Magic from Intuition

In 1988, I saw the Joffrey Ballet perform Millicent Hodgson and Kenneth Archer's reconstruction of Vaslav Nijinsky's revolutionary performance of Igor Stravinsky's *Le Sacre du Printemps* (*Rite of Spring*). I was completely taken with the music. The next day, I went to find a recording of the score and ended up with one by the Detroit Symphony Orchestra conducted by Antal Dorati—one sadly not available any more. I listened to it every day during my warm-up in the studio—a time to maintain my technical discipline but a time also to allow myself to drift into streams of consciousness. Since I exercise in an organic progression I have designed for myself, and I know what comes next in the series, my imagination can float freely.

But as I listened to *Sacre*, I found myself adding things to the warm-up—a deep shuddering in my torso and abdomen, my body responding to the extreme range of the tympani and the strings. Soon enough, I realized that I was choreographing *Sacre* not to the scenario devised by Nijinsky and Sergei Diaghilev but to the arc of the music itself. This became *State of Darkness*—completed in 1988.

It was through the texture of the score that I entered the music and knew intuitively what to choreograph. I called the work *State of Darkness* to suggest that the figure—representing both male and female, ghost and animal—takes a ritual journey out of the primal state of darkness into light. To map it, I followed an innate voice that grasped the underlying aspects of the music.

Odd things would happen in the studio. One occurred in the winter. I liked to work without artificial lights, and one day in the shadows I was sure I was visited by Nijinsky himself, who revealed that he had wished to choreograph the entire work as a solo but hadn't been allowed to. I knew it was possible for one person to take on the shifting states of the music and so I experimented with changing who I was while dancing. Sometimes I was in the spirit world, sometimes in the animal, sometimes in the present. I was constantly shifting personae, exiting my sense of self and becoming 'other'.

The costume was a simple pair of black tights. With my bare torso, small yet strong body and short hair, I appeared androgynous to many people. While the solo came to mean different things in different cultures, most women across the world felt that it was very empowering for all women and supported my endeavours wholeheartedly. A few women and some men, however, seemed to feel that to be on stage alone with this monumental work was not right for a woman.

State of Darkness has many passages choreographed around the idea of fear and courage, from entering the shadows and delighting in an animal presence to being extremely powerful to being totally out of control. I am in dialogue with the music, sometimes 'dictating' what happens next in the score by anticipating rhythmic changes and accents before they happen, and at other times being responsive to accent changes after they occur. It is a very direct give-and-take from score to choreography.

I choreographed *State of Darkness* with belief in the 'rightness' of it and in the truth of the body in the music. With that certainty I summoned 'my buddy Igor' to help me make it through each performance, to withstand and transcend the demands of the dance by helping me find the stamina and endurance I needed. I always had the sound monitors on stage up to almost full volume so that the area shuddered under the power of the music. I had to rise to that power and I wanted its full presence. The vibrations would come through the floor, enter through my feet and fill me with knowledge of the enormity of the sound.

A friend said to me once before a performance, 'I can't believe that you have to climb that mountain each time.' But I was addicted to it, to the challenge and great reward that dancing it brought. At the last crash of the music, where in the *Sacre* the Chosen One is killed by the falling of the axe, this modern woman steps out into the light, intact, strong and alive.

In the first few passages of *Black Boy* (1945), author Richard Wright describes a horrific fire caused by the carelessness of a young boy who, once his mother realizes he is still alive, is beaten to within an inch of his life. During his recovery, as he falls in and out of consciousness, the few images that keep coming into focus are those of nature—nature that is beautiful, wondrous and awe-inspiring. I'm inspired by the ability of this young child, surrounded by adversity and Jim Crow America, to be awe-struck by natural beauty and natural occurrence. In response I made *Waiting for Rain*, as a state we are always in: rain is coming—it is inevitable and it is cleansing.

> Waiting for rain—
> The sun went down,
> Tomorrow brought us
> Rain
>
> (Baldwin 1978: 584)

I have also made many dances to Philip Glass' music over the past 25 years, including scores ranging from early works such as *Music in Twelve Parts* to the later *Dreaming Awake*.

I choreograph by first listening to the score I'm interested in during my daily training. Soon I find that I am making new moves to it, which eventually become more conscious. I work very free-associatively at first—phrases of movement appear intuitively, then become linked; every movement is written down in a list I refer to later as I start to work the piece through. I listen continuously to the music, looking for the emotional thread of the score, working sometimes within the rhythmic structure, finding points to foreshadow or reference. Each moment needs to be vital and has to allow for intuition—if something 'feels' right then it usually is.

The metaphorical place where the dance is to occur gets mapped into spatial zones. Once these spatial patterns are set, the intent of the work starts to reveal itself to me. The phrases then get memorized and danced in real time. As memory gets settled and imprinted, the dance starts to take on a life of its own. It is at this point when, in turn, the patterned movement reveals its intelligence and rules that the art work reflects back to the dancer an understanding of itself and of how it should be danced.

When I dance *Provenance Unknown*, I visualize a temporal and spatial landscape populated by memory. As the dance evolves, the dancer resurrects the past and layers the landscape with the present. The cumulative effect of memories and states of being imprint the space.

Dreaming Awake is composed of two dreams, each half the score. Both dreams have their own set of themes and motifs, until the end of the second dream when a few memories of the first resurface. Here, as elsewhere, I try to create an experiential feeling of terrain through the movements, patterns and rhythms, a specific geo-psychological environment that develops through the relationship of the moving bodies to the volume of the theatre space.

Geo-psychological Space

The studio I had at the American Academy of Rome for six months in 2008 was a detached space with a skylight and high windows—it allowed for light to enter but no details of the city. This space, traditionally used for sculpting and painting, was transformed for me into a beautiful dance floor with mirrors along one side. It was an ethereal space, with ghosts of sculpture, which was all I thought about while I was there making *Cosmati Variations*.

I was at the academy to study the Cosmati mosaics. These mosaics date from the eleventh to twelfth centuries and can be seen in many of the cathedrals and churches of Rome. The mosaic designs are characterized by squares, parallelograms and circles of dark marble often contained in ribbons of lighter-coloured glass. I 'borrowed' the designs for their patterns through space as inspiration for dancers' movement.

As I researched the mosaics, I was struck by how their ribbon form was suggestive of the spine of the body, like bends in the river of the body—the *tribhanga* or S curve of Indian sculpture. The mosaics also form triangular shapes and these struck me as analogous to the body's two triangles, one created by the pelvic girdle and the other by the collarbone/solar plexus. I perceived that the structural forms of the human body were, in fact, echoed in the mosaics.

I went to the cathedral closest to the American Academy that had Cosmati floor mosaics. I measured some; all were nearly 3 feet in diameter. They also had a cropped-eyelet design that implied a circle, though an incomplete one, and a space bordered by a recumbent T. These forms conjured up relaxed geometry—repeating patterns that evolve rather than remain identical over time, patterns that leave an opening for shifts outside the pattern. I used all these elements as inspiration, composing movement phrases that took three feet of space to accomplish.

The phrases I began to compose were also populated by my interpretations of the Greek, Roman and Etruscan sculptures I was seeing every day, drawing on the body positions and poses particularly of the friezes. These sculptures presented an 'idyllic human body' with qualities of balance, regularity and symmetry. I sought to capture the poses and draping of the human body in iconic repose. Together, these sources became the basis of a new movement vocabulary.

Cosmati Variations was set to the music of John Cage—the 'First Construction' and 'Second Construction', percussion scores composed in the early 1940s. For me, the music resonated with the sound of a soldier's goosestep striding down an avenue, replete with crackling and echo. I often thought of the mosaics as silent witnesses to the centuries of dramatic historical events as well as the ceaseless continuity of time—witnesses to time held in serpentine mystery.

I began to formally organize the movement material using recurring rhythms and physical images in a nested structure. It is inside these forms that I felt I could find a link between the inner space of the dancer's mind and the outer space that the dancer moves through. As the dancer dances through a design, a sense of beauty and inspiration emerge, disclosing a hidden order.

Works Cited

FENOLLOSA, Ernest, and Ezra Pound. 1916. *'Noh' or Accomplishments: A Study of the Classical Stage of Japan*. London: Macmillan.

BALDWIN, James. 1978. *Just Above My Head*. New York: Delta Trade Paperbacks.

IMAGE 16 *State of Darkness* (1988); Molissa Fenley in photo session in New York. Photograph by Jack Mitchell © 1988.

The Sovereign Soloist: States of Exceptional Labour and *State of Darkness*

Richard Move

> The connotation of courage, which we now feel to be an indispensable quality of the hero, is in fact already present in a willingness to act and speak at all, to insert one's self into the world and begin a story of one's own.
>
> Hannah Arendt (1998: 186)

Introduction

In 1988, Molissa Fenley began a story of her own. She disbanded her internationally known ensemble, Molissa Fenley and Dancers, wore a simple costume of black tights, disrobed from the waist up and danced, as a soloist, the entirety of Igor Stravinsky's 1913 *Le Sacre du Printemps*. This 33-minute work, *State of Darkness*, was presented after performing a full first act of excerpted solos from previously choreographed ballets, *Esperanto* (from 1985) and *Second Sight* (Part Two of her three-part *Eureka*, from 1982). Before touring worldwide, *State of Darkness* premiered on 20 June 1988 at the American Dance Festival at Duke University's Reynolds Auditorium. Anna Kisselgoff, then chief dance critic for the *New York Times*, appropriately titled her review of Fenley's tour de force solo a 'Rite of Passage' and declared, 'As a dancer who has been unmatched on the experimental scene for her explosive, even primal energy, Miss Fenley has found her true center here, and challenges the pounding rhythms of Stravinsky's music with contemporary originality and fervor' (1988: n.p.).

Fenley's *State of Darkness* is an exemplary site of the political potential of dance. It resists societal constructs of labour, conventional expressions of gender and is an exceptional, uniquely contemporary reading of the score, differentiating it from other interpretations. It is also a dance with an unusually individual temporality, concurrently traversing time, of its own moment while also linked to the historicity of the original 1913 Ballets Russes production and its choreographer, Vaslav Nijinsky.

The Labour of *State of Darkness*

The central themes of Hannah Arendt's *The Human Condition* and the key terms she employs, such as 'courage', 'action' and the 'highest and greatest achievements of man' (1998: 175, 207) all resonate with *State of Darkness* as the audience bears witness to a heroic artistic feat made boldly evident by the athleticism and strength of Fenley's unequalled solo adventure. Her bare torso accentuated and progressively revealed increasing perspiration and made both visible and audible its demand for more oxygen. In the last two climactic minutes there is no repose, no respite and no slowing down just as the score dictates. Fenley accelerates with lightning-speed foot work, a dizzying multitude of spins, leaps and turns in attitude and arabesque, all intensified by her signature, expressively eloquent torso. Despite the high volume and power of the score, one hears the landing of each jump, the sounds of her bare feet turning on the black stage floor and her respiration. The spectator is forced to quickly follow her as she conquers the entirety of the stage space with continuous changes of direction, executed with rigorous precision and extreme velocity.

As Arendt describes, '[T]his precisely is the case of laboring, an activity in which man is neither together with the world nor with other people, but alone with his body, facing the naked necessity to keep himself alive' (1998: 44). I believe that Fenley's creative compulsion to re-imagine the notoriously intricate score as a solo act was born out of artistic necessity and is the motivating force that 'keeps *herself* alive'.

Fenley exhibits the surplus labour of dance with virtuosic, extraordinary stamina, evoking a palpable 'naked necessity'. This made each performance a participatory event for the audience, congruent to cultural theorist and dancer Randy Martin's description of such occurrences: 'As event, audience-as-participation cannot see or observe itself from without but its labor that, through its association and expenditure, enables the event to occur' (1998: 38). And, as Martin asserts, 'Participation springs from the disruptive potential, an indeterminacy of representation internal to the performance' (ibid.: 39). Fenley's peerless transmission of energy elicited this participatory, event-like response from those who were witness to the performance, apparent in the repeated references, in each of the numerous reviews I've read of the work, to standing ovations.

State of Darkness also illustrates dance historian and theorist John Martin's concept of the metakinetic,[1] with its combination of the powerful sonics of the score and the equally powerful soloist, producing a forceful neuromuscular affect and kinetic empathy circulating between, around and through both Fenley and the spectators. By pushing the limits of what a body can do, *State of Darkness* transformed both Fenley and her audience by the conclusion of each performance-event and, to borrow Mark Franko's turn of phrase, all became 'e/motional' (2002: 9).

Fenley was well known by the time of this premiere for her iconoclastic, ornate vocabulary emphasizing an extremely idiosyncratic use of her upper body. Her arms, often in a hyper-extended expanse, become wing-like appendages. Her hands, alternating between flattened, splayed, circular or triangular shapes, frequently shield or cover her face in a stylized manner. This sumptuous use of the upper body, propelled by high-speed patterns of repeated travelling steps, runs, sudden leaps and surprising turns, is most often initiated by the head with a whiplash-like centrifugal force. Art critic and historian RoseLee Goldberg, in *Performance Art: From Futurism to the Present,* described Fenley's vocabulary as

> A whirlwind discourse on the placement of the arms, heads and hands [. . .] she appropriated from an image bank of dance movements that suggested an Egyptian hieroglyph, or a frieze of Greek Warriors; palms were turned up as in Indian Classical Dance, or an elbow was crooked as in a Balinese curtsey, while a hip movement might recall a popular samba [. . .]. The sheer physicality of the work made it both demanding for the dance specialist and delightful for a larger audience (1998: 203).

Fenley's transcontinental childhood and adolescence contributed greatly to these bountiful allusions of global dance forms. Fenley was raised in Ithaca, New York, and was six years old when her family moved to Ibadan, Nigeria. She then attended high school in Spain before returning to the United States. Fenley recounts:

> [As] a young girl, growing up in Ibadan, Nigeria, I saw an enormous amount of Yoruban dance—dance that took place at all times of the day and night, dance made in celebration of the passages of human life, for puberty or marriage, for birth or for death. I experienced the dances with young eyes, immeasurably excited and engaged, watching everything, taking everything in, storing it for the future.[2]

Fenley's witnessing of dance as ritual and her storing of this embodied knowledge inherently informed the development of her personal and highly codified vocabulary. Along with her remarkable swiftness and astonishing stamina, Fenley's body of work reaches an apotheosis with *State of Darkness*.

The Exceptional and Sovereign Act of the Soloist

As philosopher Jacques Ranciere describes in *Dissensus*, '[S]ociety is made up of groups tied to specific modes of doing, to places in which these occupations are exercised, and to modes of being corresponding to these occupations and these places' (2010: 36). Fenley boldly defied such hegemonic modes of being. Specifically, the traditional dance-company model, organized by a single choreographer directing a group of dancers. This common structure of labour becomes a conflated and autonomous entity with Fenley's gesture of independence. Thus, it is exemplary of Franko's definition of the choreo-political and what it means to stand outside the 'persuasive kinesthetic and visual means by which individual identities are called or hailed to larger group formations' (2007: 14). This is especially significant in Fenley's case, after having first directed a group of dancers and attaining the highest levels of honours, awards, press, presentations in the most prestigious international venues and all other measures the field considers representative of the successful dance company.

In *Critical Moves,* Randy Martin posits 'mobilization' as a key principle in defining the political impact intrinsic to dance. Martin expands on this principle with 'the mobilization of participation', the 'gathering of bodies' and the 'sense of time and space [that] is generated through social life' (1998: 5, 9, 35). Martin's references are, of course, to social formations of more than one person. Fenley brazenly opposed this specific idea of mobilization and the customary dance-company model at the very height of her group's achievements, making the omniscience of the art form's institutional apparatus all the more visible by resisting both Martin's definition of mobilization and the prevailing business plan operating within the arts. As she wrote:

> To choreograph and perform this work as a soloist meant that I had to turn off a lot of the grumblings that were around me, some vocal people in the dance world who thought this

undertaking was unbelievably arrogant, and, to follow a new career as a soloist, seen as diminutive to an ensemble form, a definite step in the wrong direction.

For Martin, social mobilization and group participation are the central premise of dance as political action. Fenley's solo gesture may, at first, seem in opposition to Martin's viewpoint. But a closer look reveals that she is participating with both Nijinsky and Stravinsky the score, the rich historicity of the work and the aforementioned event-like participation of the audience—all of which generate a community and a similarly powerful and political mobilization of persons.

Perhaps Fenley did not seek to escape these normative conditions for any reason other than the 'naked necessity' of her own artistic impulse to find a new means of expressing her exacting, aesthetic vision. 'Sovereign is he,' wrote political theorist Carl Schmitt in 1922, 'who decides on the exception' (quote in Franko 2007: 21). With *State of Darkness,* Fenley decidedly named herself both the exception and the sovereign. Analogous to Franko's writing on Isadora Duncan, Fenley's *State of Darkness* may be regarded as 'an act of public display, unveiling hidden nature as prior to or intrinsically outside society, from *elsewhere*, by definition' (ibid.: 23). Like Duncan, Martha Graham, Doris Humphrey and other early modern dance pioneers, Fenley unveiled and embodied, 'revolutionary ardor and energy through an aggressive occupation of space and an energetic acknowledgement of a body's right to flow' (Franko 2002: 33). Accordingly, with *State of Darkness*, Fenley emerges as Arendt's heroine, 'a uniquely distinct "who" can become tangible *ex Postfacto* through action' (1998: 186).

Le Sacre du Printemps and *State of Darkness*

Fenley redefines what Stravinsky and Nijinsky may have intended by transforming and moulding herself, solo, into her own image of the ballet's central figure of the 'Chosen One'. Thus, her *State of Darkness* may be viewed as contrary to the original intent of the ballet's narrative, as it forcefully seeks, with full aesthetic, corporeal and political agency, to push her body to its very limit in order to affectively transmit her contemporary reading of the infamously complex and polyrhythmic score. Consequently, Fenley's version of *Rite of Spring* transcends that of the long and ever-increasing list of choreographers who have staged their own versions, from Martha Graham to Maurice Bejart and Paul Taylor, all of whom may exhibit a degree of poetic license but essentially remain true to the well-known narrative of the Ballets Russes original. 'For example,' Franko states, 'Pina Bausch's [...] *Rite of Spring* recasts the seminal ballet story as a battle of the sexes much more explicitly than does the original. This raised, at least for the American public, the question of Bausch's gender politics' (2007: 15). However, Bausch only elaborated upon this already existing and widely known element of the ballet's narrative. There is no sacrificial virgin and no male presence in the framework of Fenley's interpretation within which to place her Chosen One. Instead, she may be seen as sacrificing herself to her own choreo-political muse by emphatically *not* dancing to her own death. Her Chosen One dances towards glory, life, out of the state of darkness and into the light, something made exceedingly clear in the work's final, triumphant moment. In Fenley's own words: 'At the last crash of the music, where in the *Rite of Spring* scenario, the Chosen One is killed by the falling of the axe, this modern woman steps out into the light: intact, strong and alive.'

Fenley pronounced herself the sovereign, Chosen One, as no one before her had dared take on the score as soloist with such volition. In this way, the ballet both works with and against the historiography of the original and of the numerous subsequent interpretations and claims its own temporality. By doing so, Fenley demonstrates what Franko refers to as, '[T]he presence of a work from the past that acts as a goal for a heightening of the unrealized political possibilities of the original' (2002: 15). With *State of Darkness*, Fenley both makes history and critiques it.

State of Darkness then becomes a choreo-archive, for the archive in dance is never static—it may metamorphose and be reactivated. She proves that history, present and the future can be danced simultaneously and that her body is the archival document:

> I had seen the Joffrey Ballet perform their reconstruction of the Nijinsky original of *Le Sacre du Printemps*. I was completely taken with the music and went the next day to find a recording of the score [. . .]. Using the textural basis of the score then became the method of entering into the music and knowing what to choreograph. I called the work *State of Darkness* for precisely the reason that I didn't follow the scenario of the *Rite of Spring*. Instead, I followed an inner, intuitive voice that understood the music.

By focusing on the score as generative source for the work, she seems to explicitly evoke Nijinsky, Stravinsky and the Ballets Russes at the same time as she counters the vast *oeuvre* of *Rite of Spring* interpretations. Fenley's reading both escapes *from* and escapes *with* this weight of history, thus exhibiting the trans-temporality of her work and, most especially, this canonic dance.

State of Darkness is a sacrifice made to the dance itself, 'a giving of a dancer to herself, her public, her art' (Kisselgoff 1988: n.p.). Fenley's sacrifice is the full giving of her body and psyche required to execute this demanding work. However challenging the dance is to perform, Fenley is in no way victimized by its difficulty. Hence, it is a feminist act as well. In retrospect, Fenley says:

> In the subsequent years of performing the work as a woman on stage meant different things in different cultures. Throughout the world, most women felt that it was very empowering for all women and supported my endeavors wholeheartedly. Some others and some men seemed to feel that this was not the place for a woman.

Gender Politics

Fenley's short, cropped hair, inconspicuous maquillage, sculpted muscularity and small, exposed breasts reveal both her womanhood and her deviation from normative conventions of femininity. Fenley's queering display of gender may also be recognized as emblematic of

American identity, in that this concept has been idealistically defined by the freedom and agency to constitute the individual as self-made person. 'Whether we call it appropriation, accommodation, or collaboration, the artist's politics are frequently compounded by the situation of the woman artist in the twentieth century who both manipulated her own image and suffered its manipulation by forces beyond her control' (Franko 2002: 13). Fenley is acutely aware of the creation of her image and self-consciously constructs her presentation of a gendered self. Although referring to Mark Morris' cross-dressed roles in his *Dido and Aeneas*, Fenley's solo also elucidates Franko's statement that '[T]he sex/gender politics in which this dance engages is also therefore engaged with a politics of dance history expressed in, by and through choreography' (2007: 15). Fenley's expression of gender is especially undiluted as soloist, as there are no others around her to detract from her sex/gender choreographic display.

In dance scholar Helene Marquie's analysis of Alain Buffard's work *Dispositif 3.1* (2001) and its play on conventions of gender roles implicit in the work's title (which references philosopher Louis Althusser's concept of the *Dispositif* as defining all hegemonic forces, including those constructing societal perceptions of gender), Marquie cites '[A] certain undifferentiated state of the subject; an abandonment of the identity of the biological sexes, a momentary abolition of the dualism that rules, institutes and instrumentalizes bodies, desires' (2007: 240). Marquie asserts, however, that 'sexual identity is not abandoned' (ibid.). It is this dualism that best describes the corporal image of Fenley, who acknowledges that 'She would appear androgynous to some, small yet strong-bodied, with short hair.'

Fenley and Dance Pedagogy

Further demonstrative of Fenley's unique political manoeuvres is her defiant resistance to the obedience most often present in dance pedagogy and her deliberate choice of training methodology. Franko asserts, 'When we speak of dance and politics, we speak of the power of dance to make and unmake identities. Because dance molds the body and its way of moving, it cannot help but propose models of subjectivity in either an affirmative or negative sense' (2002: 16). Fenley publicly resisted traditional dance training while embarking upon her career in the late 1970s. Instead of the established model of taking class under the tutelage of a maestro, Fenley opted to develop her own regimen, executed daily in solitude, combining exercises culled from ballet and modern techniques, with an equal emphasis on aerobic and weight training, in order to manufacture the body necessary to execute her work. Consequently, Fenley operated, from the onset, outside the extant apparatus of the dance world's rules and regulations that choreograph the art form's most common training customs. As Deborah Jowitt describes, 'Her body sleek and trim and powerfully muscled, is not elegant in the sense that the contemporary ballet dancer's body is. She looks more like a triathlete, the aerobic-ideal of health-conscious America' (1988: 371).

In fact, the genesis of *State of Darkness* emerged first from the musical accompaniment to Fenley's daily technical ritual:

> I was just listening to the recording everyday while doing my warm-up in the studio [. . .]. I found myself adding things to the warm-up: deep shuddering in my torso and abdominals, and watching my body respond to the extremes of tympani and the strings. Soon enough, I realized that I was choreographing to the work, choreographing to the piece of music, not to the scenario devised by Nijinsky and Diaghilev.

Dancing *with* Nijinsky, Stravinsky and Others

Leaps, balances on relevé, attitudes, arabesques, battements and other identifiably balletic movements constitute the piece's vocabulary, although never in the classical sense, as Fenley's execution is simply too idiosyncratic to reduce movement to such easily discernible terminology. Some of the work's most striking moments lie in its strategically situated episodic tremors, spasmodic quivers and convulsive contractions, all in direct visceral reaction to the psychophysical impulses evoked by the score. Jenn Joy's examination of the choreographic spasm

IMAGE 17 *State of Darkness* (1988); Molissa Fenley in rehearsal at Battery Dance Studio, New York. Photograph by Chantal Regnault © 1988.

illuminates Fenley's spasmodic dance-making: 'As a movement of thought, the spasm interrogates the visual through the kinetic, the body through language, expression through emotion, performer through witness, pain through pleasure' (2009: 67). These moments articulate new possibilities of communication—they seem involuntary at first, but ultimately the viewer understands them to be deliberate leitmotifs, choreographed and repeated with each performative instantiation. These spasm-like moments create their own choreo-political space, as they are of equal import to the leaps, turns and high legs most commonly considered the defining gestures of dance, affectively arousing in Fenley and the spectator a 'longing to trespass into a body and onto the stage' (ibid.: 73). It is these convulsive trespasses that conjure, for me, choreographic moments that speak directly to the phenomenological spirit transmission of the afterlives left lingering by the trans-temporal weight of the score and its countless incarnations. It evokes the theories of sociologist Avery Gordon in *Ghostly Matters* and the haunting '[s]pirits of improperly buried bodies that are always present' (2008: 18), specifically the spirit of Nijinsky, especially when contemplating the dark and painful last years of his life. Fenley exudes an intuitive engagement with these incorporealities, further elucidating that 'such endings that are not over is what haunting is about'. The work can then be seen as a choreographic invocation of the dead 'tied to historical and social effect' (ibid.: 139, 190):

> Odd things would happen in the studio, it was in the winter and I like to work with no artificial light and in the shadows of the room, I would be sure that I was being visited by Nijinsky himself who revealed that he had wished that he had choreographed the entire work as a solo but hadn't been allowed to. I knew that there was the possibility for one person to take on the varying states of the music. I experimented with changing who I was while dancing, sometimes in the spirit world, sometimes in the animal, sometimes in the present, constantly shifting personas in the dance, exiting a sense of 'self' and becoming something 'other,' being transported.

Fenley's ghostly visitations in the studio echo Andre Lepecki's double usage of the term haunting 'to emphasize choreography's capacity to invoke absent presences [. . .] to propose an epistemological accounting of the particular circulatory temporality initiated by choreography's capacity for haunting history' (2006: 28).

For Fenley, who lost a close friend to AIDS around the time she saw the Joffrey's reconstruction, the work is definitively a melancholic, cryptic cenotaph. As she stated at the moment of its creation, 'It's time now that we need a humanist point of view, because we are living in a "state of darkness." It's time we have to be vulnerable and giving' (quote in Daly 2002: 112). As Ann Daly articulated in her review in *High Performance,* 'What had always felt ritualistic in her all female ensemble works has in the solo format become palpably religious'. Fenley is dancing through landscapes of hauntings and dreams, pushing to embody the incorporeal and make it visible: 'The result *State of Darkness,* was an incantation; a rather desperate act of faith in the future of humankind' (2002: 114). The haunting presence of the ballet's originators, the persistent memory of her friend's death and the creation of the ballet at the height of the AIDS epidemic further speak to the trans-historical facet of the work, from 1913 and onward towards a utopic futurity and characterize, according to Franko, '[t]he necessary relation to the fleshly body to its markers of identity and subjectivity lends feeling its structure from experience, through performance, to interpretation. This feeling is practically unmediated in that its passage from life to stage entails no studied adaptation' (2002: 41). These presences and absences further invest the work with layers of affect fundamental to its success as a work of political choreography while further aligning Fenley with the founding figures of modern dance in the 1930s, 'who imagined modern dance's potential to stimulate social change' (ibid.: 26).

Fenley and the Frailty of Human Affairs

As Arendt states, 'Yet while the various limitations and boundaries we find in every body politic may offer some protection against the inherent boundlessness of action, they are altogether helpless to offset its second outstanding character: its inherent unpredictability' (1998: 191).

And, eventually, Fenley emerges as the fallen heroine, with her opening-night solo performance at New York's Joyce Theater on 7 October 1995, when she collapsed to the floor 20 minutes into the opening solo. The curtain was closed and the rest of the season was cancelled due to a serious knee injury. Critic Terry Trucco wrote in the *New York Times*, 'In her 20-year career, much of it spent as a solo performer, the choreographer and dancer had never missed a performance and had never been seriously injured. As she herself put it recently, "I considered myself invincible"' (1995: n.p.). Fenley remembered, '"Lying there, I felt I'd never dance again," she said. "I thought, they might as well shoot me, like a horse." And she recalled her doctor's remark, "You're 40. Aren't you at the end of your career anyway?"' (ibid.). An unfortunately common and callous reminder of the presumed life span of the dancer that exists largely outside the dance world, rife with negative connotations regarding the validity of the dancer, both as artist and productive resource within the economies of cultural labour. Inside the dance world, however, there are countless practitioners whose greatness is regularly presented publicly literally decades beyond this doctor's (and the general public's) perceptions of the duration of a dancer's career. One example is that of Mikhail Baryshnikov and Steve Paxton, well into their sixties and seventies, respectively, who danced clearly, confidently, strongly and beautifully, in a shared evening of solo works that premiered 19 May 2010 at New York's Baryshnikov Arts Center.

Summoning the similar resolve and 'naked necessity' that enabled Fenley to undertake *State of Darkness,* she persisted to create. Shortly after surgery, she crawled, literally, up the formidably steep, high flight of 56 stairs to the top floor of what was then the Dia Arts Foundation in Soho. There, she continued to produce. The result is *Chair Dance,* in which Fenley dances while seated in a simple wooden chair, unable to bear weight on the leg during her rehabilitation.

It seems safe to say she would never have created 'Chair Dance,' the opening section of 'Regions,' had she not been injured. Seated in a slat-back wooden armchair, a metaphor for support, Ms. Fenley performs a remarkably physical dance without almost ever touching foot to floor. Instead, she balances atop the seat, extends her arms skyward and winds herself around the armrest, 'since I couldn't wind myself around space,' she explained (ibid.).

Chair Dance and its making is another illustration of Fenley's conscious, political refusal to submit to either the subjugation of her own body, or the external forces that presumed her career would have ended with the close of the curtain that evening. A telling example of the extreme marginalization and highly unusual labour practices that are most exceptional to dance and, particularly, to the art practice and body of work that is Molissa Fenley's.

The courageous story Fenley began with *State of Darkness* again resonates with Arendt: 'To do and to suffer are like opposite sides of the same coin, and the story that an act starts is composed of its consequent deeds and sufferings' (1998: 190).

Notes

1 Dance scholar John Martin first used the term 'metakinesis' in the 1930s when he proposed theat the dance spectator first responds via the senses of sight and sound, which then become internalized in the neuromuscular system and result in kinetic empathy.

2 As dance scholar Mark Franko has stated, 'Although choreographers are not the ultimate authorities on the meaning of their work, their words should be weighted in the analysis' (2002: 11). I wholeheartedly concur and thus quote from Fenley's own writings that she shared me with through email correspondence (22 July 2010). All quotations by Fenley in this essay are, unless otherwise mentioned, from this same correspondence.

Works Cited

ARENDT, Hannah. 1998[1958]. *The Human Condition*. Chicago: University of Chicago Press.

DALY, Ann. 2002. *Critical Gestures: Writings on Dance and Culture*. Middletown, CT: Wesleyan University Press.

FRANKO, Mark. 2002. *The Work of Dance: Labour, Movement, and Identity in the 1930s*. Middletown, CT: Wesleyan University Press.

——. 2007. 'Dance and the Political: States of Exception' in Susanne Franco and Marina Nordera (eds), *Dance Discourses: Keywords in Dance Research*. London and New York: Routledge, pp. 11–28.

GOLDBERG, RoseLee. 1998. *Performance Art: From Futurism to the Present*. New York: Harry N. Abrams.

GORDON, Avery. 2008. *Ghostly Matters: Haunting and the Sociological Imagination*. Minneapolis: University of Minnesota Press.

JOWITT, Deborah. 1988. *Time and the Dancing Image*. New York: William Morrow.

JOY, Jenn. 2009. 'Anatomies of Spasm' in Andre Lepecki and Jenn Joy (eds), *Planes of Composition: Dance, Theory and the Global*. London: Seagull Books.

KISSELGOFF, Anna. 1988. 'In 'State of Darkness', a Dancer's Rite of Passage.' *New York Times*, 8 October. Available at: www.nytimes.com/1988/10/08/arts/review-dance-in-state-of-darkness-a-dancer-s-rite-of-passage.html (last accessed on 5 February 2015).

LEPECKI, Andre. 2006. *Exhausting Dance: Performance and the Politics of Movement*. New York: Routledge.

MARQUIE, Helene. 2007. 'Dispositif Trouble: When What is Said is Not Shown' in Susanne Franco and Marina Nordera (eds), *Dance Discourses: Keywords in Dance Research*. London and New York: Routledge, pp. 236–50.

MARTIN, Randy. 1998. *Critical Moves: Dance Studies in Theory and Politics*. Durham, NC: Duke University Press.

RANCIERE, Jacques. 2010. *Dissensus: On Politics and Aesthetics*. London and New York: Continuum.

TRUCCO, Terry. 1995. 'Once, She Considered Herself Invincible.' *New York Times*, 26 November. Available at: www.nytimes.com/1995/11/26/arts/dance-once-she-considered-herself-invincible.html (last accessed on 5 February 2015).

Poems

Bob Holman

The Architect of Movement

Praise Poem for Molissa Fenley

The structuralist poet of dance! She is
Molissa Fenley, first view—fire
Flies downstage on what seems

Movement itself—this is
Attack of the Firebird ouch
Sacred Spring my God my

Goodness Boing Boing!
Coming straight at me (you)!
It's all the bassoon can do to

Make a tune of a knot
An essay of a string all
The damn fiddles in the world

LEAP when it's pure dance it's pure faith
As the point of balance maintains
A compass heart and a steady North

Equidistant from the stars? Never!
Are the stars, at start a heart
On fire I would say Molissa Fenley

's Heart's on Fire not how many
Times but Now only enormous quiet
Brings you up to date memory
Simplicity when captured   isn't
                                                  quite
so
                                            simple
And dance that one back to me

OK, then level the air and sweep
The balance level, the pole beam
Stillness cataract lowering beauty

Into a vessel the size of a woman
The shape of a dance
The music of line

Her ruthless geometries
Her riotous gem gymnopedies
Her edges shear sky

No other way slanting
Perfecter perfectest
Say no more

IMAGE 18 *Trace* (1996); Molissa Fenley in performance at the Joyce Theater, New York; painting by Roy Fowler. Photograph by Julie Lemberger © 1996.

Helicopter Flower Flower Helicopter

That spring was unlike any other time I've ever experienced.
It was full of the chaos of existence, meeting strangers who
Turned out to be the lovers of former lovers, taking a job that
Immediately turned into a whole different thing, where my skills
Were actually used and I was actually paid for it. In the morning,
one cup of coffee and a cigarette and I had the whole *Times* cross-
Word done. I'd watch the City come to life as if it were a painting
That animated with the sun. The noise went from silence
To deafening in a single long crescendo, a delirious inexorable
Dance of Evolutionary participation, if not understanding.
It was all in the doing.
I wouldn't go so far as to call it joy.
But it certainly did smack of life lived at full intensity, two trees
Bending in a hurricane, totally set loose and yet fully grounded.
That kind of dance. I found myself
Repeating certain phrases when cretin images approached:
Twisting the Sky
Setting Fire to the Ocean
Lightning Strike Under Water
Finally I admitted that I was in love with K_____
The animals who had been waiting alongside the highway
All watched my gyrations as if I were their keeper

Who

who watches
who sees
who knows
who cares
who believes
who introduces
who follows
who wants to know
who couldn't care less
who understands
who starts over
who balances
who jumps
who forgets
who dashes
who realizes
who raps
who taps
who says get lost
who touches herself
who appreciates the repetition
who has inherent diversity
who wears her body on the inside
who takes you for a ride
who can't help it
who gives up
who reimagines

who flies
who lies
who brings it all whole cloth
who carouses
who stays up
who comes together
who appreciated the last drop
who winks
who blinks
who finds out
who can't believe it
who loves
who touches
who sleeps
who shares
who journeys
who incarcerates the imagination
who luckily meets another
who swings about
who terrifies
who twists
who incinerates
who lights
who puts out
who justifies
who guarantees
who leaves it well enough alone
who can't stop
who puts the best foot forward
who swirls
who resonates

who flips around and over
who stands tall
who stands still
who is alone
who gets ahold of sky
who insinuates the beat
who doesn't know
who lifts
who dives
who dries
who dies
who branches
who cries
who ever shall see
who ever is aware
who ever stands before you
in constant movement shall
create a world that
is yours alone
who enjoys
and who sings
and who brushes
and who latches
who brings rings
who swims in air
and breathes dance
who watches and takes
it all in
who stands forever finally
leaping through the window of faith

IMAGE 19 *Esperanto* (1985); Molissa Fenley, Jill Diamond in photo session in New York; costumes by Jean-Paul Gaultier. Photograph by Chris Callis © 1985.

In Church Dance

No chords heard, the balustrade full of confident spires. The stained
Glass was a-blazing, the monks vividly carousel carouse in the vaults
Like water in a cyclone jar, twirling the frankincense like a helicopter
Of flowers. Irises. Peonies. Petals flashingly floating by. Total
Immersion in the sacred laws, revelling in Total Freedom as defined
By that movement which embraces God as the Body and never the other
Way round, and then the Other Way Round and about and did you hear
The plain song chant that built to a climax of union—
a lost note becoming
The dance itself, can you hear the dance with your eyes now Helicopter
Flower the church engulfed in the actual flames of salvation, burning
burning yet ever whole, unscathed, a testament of faith
a vision of profound
Balanced perfection—Stasis Absolute—fragmenting into the molecular
Particularization of Eternal Inevitability—Only the Vision Of the faithful
Shall emerge, a new understanding so full of light that drowning is
A natural state and to ascend is to comprehend the glow and blaze
Life assumes, the Last Water, normalcy at last exchanged for
The physicalization of faith adjudicating itself, one to one to one, a tree of
Music that waves its way rushing to the sea and ever returning a wave

Double Beginning

A Double Beginning

cirrus sans tsurus

Enormous quiet brought you up to date memory

A double beginning

cirrus sans tsurus

Enormous quiet brought you up to date memory

Simplicity when captured isn't

quite so

simple

Turns into fragments

Fragments fragment
Ferment Foment Repent Cement Intent
Relent Hellbent Per cent For rent
To
one's
heart's
content

In the choreography there are many stillnesses
(Like today)

Level the air and sweep the balance level

I started to make it and then my father died. Study on the subway. A foal jumps, like on TV. The hands placed over the head—a shaking leaf. Things elbowed things outta the way, hey, You! Be able To tell Time like Fela. Ni Knee Jeer EeUh. Nigeria teaches.

Don't Di-a-gon-al (the diagonal as front)

Rely on myself like you taught me. It's hard.

Blessed be the seeds you sow. Yam eyes.

Into an overall unity. Step into a step. Step step leap into willingness.

The ambience of nonchalance from somewhere else, fancy pants
Lying on la playa working hard (step) on your nonchalance

If you gotta work, it ain't workin
If yagottawork it ain't workin
Talkin bout Love ya jerk, if ya gotta work it ain't workin
& this ends the letter & I hope yr better
Half is better than none
And the one at the end says, 'Goodbye, my Friend
Gotta hit the new high before the law gets wind
Gotta hijack a convertible and blow this town
And its underground—gotta make a break
And amend the bend—recapitulate
And capsize the end—a change of perspective
The vision's receptive

Inspiring input put your foot down. Step drag step.

Bend and follow the bend to bow

Keep abruption

Too Far Out

You gotta go
Too far out
To bring back
The psychedelic boat

Once upon or twice that's nice

A hop with you on it

Can't help moving my love around

Beseech the lack of too little
are forewarned
Of the stone I say, It's a stone

might stop
pressure drop

Or in or on or on her honour or over and out

will you wish a song for this dance
placing a piece of body
incorporate the tender string in
the untuned guitar

A spot where you can change
The effortless Groucho and the slow hangman's walk into the mirror
O! birds of heavenly delight, Tweet your polyrhythmic antiphonal strophe down on me

When it's pure dance it's pure faith in the balletic leap twirl right outta there

Like a kid on a mission

I can remember the way your body curved into
Mine even as you lay dying there was a mutuality
Of skin I'll never feel again

might stop
hop
or not

might flip
or flop

it's easier
                    to follow
it's easier to follow
                                        what's going on?
it's easier to follow what's going on
                                                  it's not   going on
it's easier to follow what's going on when it's not going on

the double beginning

begins now

Now begins the double beginning!

It's a flop that flips

Might not hop

Might not stop hopping
I hope it stops
  Hop hop hop

Pressure drop
Drop drop

the untuned guitar
incorporates a tender string
places a piece of body (you wish!)
a dance for this song
a song for this dance
and now a poem for nothing

Out and over and on her
And in her or on her
Or on her honour

The stone says it's a stone
I say I'm a stone
Language is what the stones thought of
When they wanted to dance

A change of perspective—the vision's receptive
Balanced on one finger on a bowling ball
You come to the conclusion as you start to fall:
I'm fallin I'm fallin
I'm fallin fallin fallin
What now? What then?
What's up if not now when
On delay we're on delay
Andale! Andale!

It's gettin cold—we're on hold

Step step hands over head a shaking leaf

A hop with you on it

Forewarned: the lack of too little
Once upon or twice that's nice
Abruption! The ambience from somewhere else,
Nonchalance lying on la playa
Inspiring input put your foot down. Step drag step.
Bend. Follow the bend to bow
Now di-a-gon-al

And now
Your willingness leaps into overall unity. Step step.
Yam seeds. Sowing the blessed eyes.
It's hard to rely on myself like you taught me.
Teaching in Nigeria, the step and the stop step.
No jeer iger Nigeria, in Fela time.
In time, time, push through air
To tell time
Elbowing out
And a shaking leaf

A spot where you can change
The effortless Groucho and the slow hangman's walk into the mirror
O birds of heavenly delight, Tweet your polyrhythmic antiphonal
strophe down on me!
A foal jumps, like on TV. The hands placed over the head—
a shaking leaf.

When it's pure dance it's pure faith in the balletic leap twirl right
Outta there. Like a kid on a mission

cirrus sans tsurus

Enormous quiet brought you up to date memory

And I'll share it like an orange
Sectioned like a daisy
petals like a cross-town Motown
Pick it up
From another
Not quite there
But hear
The end

For Molissa Fenley, Katie McGreevy, Cassie Mey

IMAGE 20 *Praxis* (1982); Molissa Fenley in performance at the Riverside Studios, London. Photograph by Chris Harris © 1982.

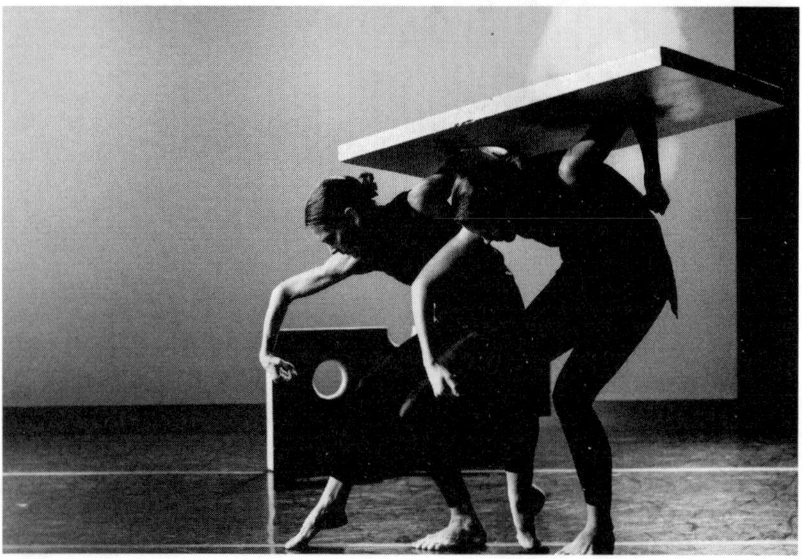

(Top) IMAGE 21 *Patterns and Expectations* (2005); Wanjiru Kamuyu, Cassie Mey, Ashley Brunning, Molissa Fenley in rehearsal at Dance Theater Workshop, New York. Photograph by Julie Lemberger © 2005. (Bottom) IMAGE 22 *Prop Dance #5* (*The Prop Dances*) (2010), Molissa Fenley, Cassie Mey in performance at Joyce Soho, New York; props by Keith Sonnier. Photograph by Julie Lemberger © 2010.

A Conversation with Tere O'Connor

Molissa Fenley

TERE O'CONNOR. I'm here with Molissa Fenley, and I want to interview you on this occasion because you say you are doing your work—can you say where you are doing your work?

MOLISSA FENLEY. At the DUMBO White Wave Festival, the first week in November, on an evening with other choreographers, and I'm performing two pieces.

O'CONNOR. I'm going to go right into some of the things. I go see a lot of work—I think you do, too—and I see that one of the things that is, maybe mistakenly, being called 'contemporary' is to not

First published in 'Critical Correspondence' on the website of Movement Research, 2005. Available at: www.movementresearch.org/criticalcorrespondence/ (last accessed on 9 November 2014).

move any more. I'm still interested in any kind of range of no movement or a lot of movement. I think all that can be part of contemporary content. I think you are doing that. You know, I've seen your work since I was really young. We're not that much older than each other, but you started working before I did, so I always looked up to what you were doing.

I'd like to talk about a couple of aspects of it, and just kind of let you freely talk. I talked to you about it in the studio the other day, about the gestures and how they are so—I call it 'runic'—or how they are . . .

FENLEY. . . . almost like an alphabet.

O'CONNOR. Like an alphabet! But an unreadable one, one that doesn't want me to read it. So there's both the 'plastic arts' of it that I'm looking at—it's visual—and the internal thing that's going on in you as a contemporary person. You know? And sometimes, in the earlier days, dressed in really cutting-edge fashion items, these blendings of contemporary and something really primitive—I've always been really interested in that. I see it as a long continuum in your work, and I would like you to talk about what you think of that—anything, from any points of view.

FENLEY. OK. Well, I think runic is a really good word for it, because there's a kind of feeling of magic that's involved in that gesturing. The gesturing evolved really early on in my career, probably during my last year of college, at Mills, where I became really interested in an Egyptian hieroglyphic-type of profile work—an archaic type of style that then, as I started working on it, morphed into the three-dimensionality of the torqueing of the torso, which became a trademark, being in a position and then torqueing and spinning out of it really fast. The body and the arms would often be initiating that force. I started codifying that more and more as time went on.

Another thing about it was having grown up in Nigeria, West Africa, and having not come to the United States until I started college—until I was 16. I lived here until I was six but my real formative years were in a third-world country. When I think back to my childhood, or when I just close my eyes and think about the imagination of that period in time in my life, often very alone—we lived sort of out and away from people, so I was always by myself in the afternoons after school—and remember having this kind of language that I devised for me and my dog . . .

O'CONNOR (*laughs*). That's great!

FENLEY. It was this sign-language thing with my dog. In a funny way, that's sort of been incorporated as well, as a knowledge that the upper body is so informed, so communicative. Then, seeing so much of Yoruban dance as a young child—the upper body is just, you know, gesturing all the time and rhythmic, and often in counterpoint to what the lower body is doing. The lower body is often transporting the body through space and the upper body is doing all this akimbo sort of stuff—that then is a language as well.

O'CONNOR. So, it's a layering of these things.

FENLEY. It's a layering of that, and then, as I said, codifying it further as I went into my career here. I was very interested in Balinese dance, Indian dance, mudra. I was never interested in the idea of learning specifically what those mudras signified, because I thought that was really not right—you just can't take from a culture . . .

O'CONNOR. No.

FENLEY. Right? And you see people do that.

O'CONNOR. Yes, they do, and that's a really interesting subject matter.

FENLEY. But seeing what was going on with the hands—because in Western dance you don't really have the hands as being almost, you know, like a fan, or this very extreme curve that can place . . .

O'CONNOR. Like the Javanese dance.

FENLEY. Right. And that's so expressive that I just fell in love with it. And that became part of the language as well. So, all of these things are part of it. And then, as with the making of each dance, I tried to dig deeper into what that language is, into finding things that are specific for a specific dance. For instance, that piece you saw the other day . . . *Dreaming Awake*.

O'CONNOR. To a Philip Glass score.

FENLEY. Yeah, a Philip Glass score that has two lives—it can be done as a solo, or as a trio performed with two of my dancers, Ashley Brunning and Cassie Mey. So, in the making of it, I made sure that the language that was chosen for that piece was very endemic to it and not from anything else. The expression of the language within that dance then starts and evolves and goes to some kind of—not necessarily fruition—but some kind of other . . .

O'CONNOR. Other place, yeah.

FENLEY. Yeah, that gets explored and dealt with.

O'CONNOR. I can really relate to what you're saying, and I think it's good for an audience to see because I could think of an audience member saying, 'Well, it looks similar to the other dances.' But I know something about being in a really micro-place, and finding the enormity of choices within that place, you know? Because I do think you have a style, but I don't think it's a place of stopping for you. I think it's . . . it's generative for you.

FENLEY. Yes, it's very true. It's a place I always cull from, a place like a reservoir that is present, where I can always go and dig something out. And when I do, I try to propel it into this new form, into another form. And often that involves either a timing issue or a spatial issue. I'm really interested in how dance is situated in space. When I worked as a soloist for so many years, that was really the whole premise—this individual in space, and what does that say about our culture. What does that say about dance itself or the individual? It's taking a stand, taking a position.

O'CONNOR. Do you think you were trying to . . . where there're inferences being made, or was it completely just a projection field for you—when you were in that place, from your point of view?

FENLEY. From my point of view, it was really about taking a stand of some sort, depending on where a work would be performed. In Japan, for instance, there was a time when a woman onstage, by herself, was unheard of. Whereas in India a woman alone onstage is like: Well, yes, why would you ever want anyone else onstage with you?

O'CONNOR. That's really interesting.

FENLEY. And then in Nigeria, a person would not stand out alone—a person would always be a part of a group. That collective space is always very present. So, to work as a soloist all that time was really a deepening of an emotional expression of a person standing alone. But emptied—I mean, I think it was never just me, Molissa Fenley, standing there. It was me as some kind of iconographic representation of a solo human being. And I think I was really quite androgynous at that point in my life and I was really interested in that. It was as if this wasn't necessarily a man, this wasn't necessarily a woman—this was a person at large within a space. I learnt a lot from that period.

O'CONNOR. Yeah, I think it's an extrapolation of a basic root metaphor of dance—the human figure is used to be projected upon. I mean, you can't necessarily be as specific as you can in a narrative realm, so the human figure becomes a kind of adhesive for all the suggestions coming from the minds of the viewer. I feel like that was very evocative in those solo works.

FENLEY. When you think of ancient art, it's the sculpture that really exists over time. I've been very interested in ancient sculpture. Sometimes, in periods of my life, I would just go to the museums and take those stands—particularly the Asian sculpture, the top body is going this way, the hips are going that way and the legs are going another way. It's as if the body is a river, a flowing object, and to me that's a tie-in. Cycladic art I absolutely adore—these really iconic, graphic positions of the arms, particularly, or of the body just being one entity.

O'CONNOR. Can you tell me what that brings you, when you go there and relate to them? Because the other day I was talking to you about the relationship of what I saw as runic with the temporal setting that you create, which comes from a kind of twentieth-century knowledge, certainly—and related to a lot of twentieth-century music—but also this idea of continuum. Maybe a post-minimalist look at time. How do those relate? I don't know if you know the answer to that—I think it's something you are working on. Because if you are standing still . . . when you stand still, is it electrifying? Does it generate forward movement through time somehow for you? What do you think about that?

FENLEY. Do you remember a work called *Bardo*?

O'CONNOR. I do! About the 49 days after the death . . .

FENLEY. *Bardo* had a lot of stillness in it, yet within that stillness there was the sense that this metabolic body is continuing and that our sense of watching is continuing. It's taking that stillness of the body and the stillness of the person watching, and maybe together going somewhere.

I think that stillness allows for an entrance that doesn't happen through the continuum of dancing. In my early work, when the dancing was constantly 'going', that was really my interest in that period, particularly with group work—that there would always be this feeling that space was being emptied and filled, that there was this ongoing-ness . . . . An area of the space would be taken by one dancer, that dancer would leave, it would be alluded to by someone else, in an inverse relationship to what the other person had just done—maybe an arc was described, then another dancer performed its inverse or performed it smaller or larger or in the air or on the floor.

O'CONNOR. I want to go back to the other thing, but now you're talking about that time in those early works, like *Hemispheres*, etc. I always felt it was a problem—or a stopping point—that people looked at it and equated it with sport, athleticism or aerobics.

FENLEY. That's horrible! (*Laughs.*)

O'CONNOR. It's so much more interesting than that. I always thought that was a block . . . for the work.

FENLEY. Well, you know, the politics of criticism. That's a whole other issue.

O'CONNOR. Yes. And marketing. But I think that's something people glommed onto, and I think it's good if it can get your work out there. But I thought, 'You're missing a whole layer of this!'

FENLEY. Yeah. I remember it was like, 'Oh, you could be the Jane Fonda of dance.' There are so many issues to talk about with that. I would have people tell me that I made them feel embarrassed about their bodies. I had trained myself to a point where doing a dance like *Hemispheres* was a piece of cake. Remember the three of us—Silvia [Martins], Scottie [Mirviss] and I?

O'CONNOR. Of course!

FENLEY. The three of us danced the work all night long, and then it was like, 'OK, now what?!' We were absolutely women of steel!

O'CONNOR. But that was secondary to the subject matter of it.

FENLEY. Absolutely! Because if you train your body to a point where that kind of physical work is effortless, it's a physical relationship to your mind. It's all about concentration, it's all about discipline and how to filter your mind into zeroing in on the body. So it was really metaphysical.

O'CONNOR. You're relocating continuum through this.

FENLEY. Absolutely. A few people would get it.

O'CONNOR. I got it! I was so into it, you know?

FENLEY. Yeah. And when we did *Hemispheres* again at the Kitchen just recently, to re-enter that, 25 years later . . .

O'CONNOR. Oh my god!

FENLEY. . . . in my 50s.

O'CONNOR. That's intense. You went to it from a mind exercise, so it didn't necessarily have to be . . .

FENLEY. I mean, yeah, you have to get to it physically, but you get there through your mind, whereas when you're younger, you just sort of forge ahead, and you have this amazing musculature that can deal with it! To do that kind of work, later in years—like right now I'm reconstructing *State of Darkness*, I'm going to be setting it on Pacific Northwest Ballet [PNB].

O'CONNOR. You're not going to . . .

FENLEY. Well, I could! That's what is amazing!

O'CONNOR. *State of Darkness* is Molissa's version of *The Rite of Spring*, which she danced topless—it was beautiful. I saw it in Florence, if you remember.

FENLEY. That was the absolute premiere of the piece—and Enzo [Celli] got so mad!

O'CONNOR. He got mad?

FENLEY. Yeah, remember? He and . . . um . . . Enzo and Guy—what was his name? Bartolucci?

O'CONNOR. Oh, Giuseppe Bartolucci.

FENLEY. Yeah, had a huge fight with you about it, because they both hated it and you loved it.

O'CONNOR. Oh! Right! I remember that! Well, you know, in Italy, that's not called a fight—that's called a debate.

FENLEY. Well, I mean, it was great—it was really super fun. Anyway, I'm doing that again, and for the PNB. I asked Peter Boal, who is the director at PNB, 'Are you going to have the women not wear shirts?' And he said, 'No, because then it'd just be called the "topless ballet".' It's interesting that the first thing you said was that the piece was done topless. To me—and this is another aspect about having grown up in Nigeria, where we just never wore shirts—it was not a big deal. You'd often see a woman's breasts and it was never . . . anything.

O'CONNOR. No, I didn't mean to characterize it, I'm just bringing some anecdotal information to it.

FENLEY. Yeah, I know, but it is a thing that becomes an endemic thing. It's, you know, 'Oh, *that* ballet.'

O'CONNOR. Let's get back to where we were. I'm interested in the relationship of the runic thing or something plastic—I call it—and solid, to continuum or what I was describing as this post-minimalist thing. We've talked about it as being from the molecular body, or the moving internal body, but I think it posits something about the relationship to objects around you in the world. For people, that's really important. To say something about that object that is moving past me, or I'm moving around, and the sensation changing—the whole language of dance that I think is really present in your use of the plastic versus the trajectory of time passing.

FENLEY. I think that might also have to do with the spatial concepts that we're talking about—the body moving around objects that are invisible, setting up sculptural designs on the stage that are then . . . that the body sort of moves through to continue.

O'CONNOR. It's a relationship I look at in many people's work, and I ask, 'Are they adept at this, or not?' 'Are they even aware of it?' I think it's a good thing to talk about because—going back to the politics of criticism—I think a lot of criticism is based only on the visual and on stopped imagery, as opposed to the fact that those images are in a temporal setting. They're moving by you relative to one another. So, the ways that we do that form the whole language. It's a really interesting thing to investigate, and I think you are one of the people investigating it by taking dance and really committing to it as a valid form of research. So each piece you do examines that thing, you know? It is difficult to talk about but I think that something like . . . I forget what piece it was—it was a while back, and you did it at the Joyce, and there were these attachments to your body . . .

FENLEY. *331 Steps.*

O'CONNOR. . . . and I thought there was an attempt there to visualize something that was going on spatially—like rays emanating. And sometimes I feel like there's a circularity, a spinning three-dimensionality to what you are trying to do there, and that that generates a time sense also.

FENLEY. That piece had to do with being attached to the back wall by a long piece of cloth while trying to manoeuvre your steps. The idea was that you get caught up with other people's attachments and you have to move around, underneath or above them. But I think this temporal thing is really interesting. The vocabulary changes a lot according to the speed. You're talking about how a lot of dance isn't really dance any more, that there are images which are made, image against another image's place. Whereas the transitional moments are really almost not even adhered to—or thought of—as being important. I think my work rarely gets to a moment where you say, 'OK, that's a second,' or 'Stop!'

O'CONNOR. Something that's readable.

FENLEY. I use stillness but in a very different way. The continuum thing means that all the movement necessarily has an equal value, or equal validity, to it, so that you're not making pictures—you're making motion that of course is made up of pictures but that is continuing over time. That, I think, puts your mind into a different place as you watch dance. You have a reading of time passing over a period of time rather than the dramatic effect of something being placed. The effect, I think, is cumulative . . .

O'CONNOR. I agree.

FENLEY. . . . of the temporal work. As time passes, the experience of being there, present, watching—the experience of dancing it at that level of commitment—that's where it goes someplace else.

O'CONNOR. Right.

FENLEY. And I think that's kind of transformative. I think that's a kind of magic thing that goes back to the runic concept.

O'CONNOR. It's also a desire you have to reorganize time.

FENLEY. To something that is outside our normal realm. Because to me that's what the theatre should be—you go in and you are outside your normal realm. For things that take place over real time, you have a half an hour or something. Within that, you have time-travel, you have past, present, future. Time varies according to how deeply one is dancing and how deeply one is watching. It's an even match—it has to be. I think, in a way, audiences are not trained to do that any more.

O'CONNOR. Unfortunately.

FENLEY. I think that is a very sad thing. You know how we were saying the other day that the piece teaches you how to watch it while you watch it?

O'CONNOR. Yeah, if you can let go that.

FENLEY. If you can let go that, yeah. And I think that's true of many art forms. You go to a sculpture show by John Chamberlain, for instance, and there are all these hedges of cars stacked together, and you see it as a visual entity, as an iconographic thing. Yet it's in the making of it and in the understanding of its components and what it means—and you know a little bit about the person who made it, you know?—that it becomes a full experience. Or you can come in and say, 'Oh it's a bunch of cars.' So it has to do with engaging—how deeply does an audience want to engage? And I think they do! I think that if you give people something that is engaging, they are usually happy to be engaged.

O'CONNOR. I think so too.

FENLEY. I think people love to read, people love poetry, film. I think our culture likes to think that they don't, because it's more marketable to be quick—let's be quick . . .

O'CONNOR. Also, the kind of criteria for a product—an element that is stopped and doesn't move in time—is hoisted onto this temporal setting. Even at the image level, people look for a product—

what's that one thing that is capturable, something that I can use to denote that experience.

FENLEY. Right—a logo.

O'CONNOR. Logo-setting, which becomes a temporal idea, because you are looking for a stopping point as you watch it. And if you're offering to the world another temporal ideology, it's going to have to be filtered through that, somehow.

I think that even people who are doing what they would call 'outer edge'—I can think of a range of different people—they always have to be aware of how their time is kneaded out, and what the inference is of the way they are using time. It has meaning, the way you are using time, the density of elements within that amount of time, and it's inescapable. And I really would love for choreographers to redouble their attention to that, because there's an issue of how and why people are coming to it with that is different from what it was when we started, you know? I really see that change—it can be so powerful.

I also wanted to talk to you about some of the endings you had, which I think are so lovely. You can say that you just stop in some of them but they're arrived at. I'm thinking of one where you just do a *plié* and you finish in an attitude. Does that ring a bell?

FENLEY. I came up in an attitude and that was the end?

O'CONNOR. Yeah, that's the end. It's just like, 'dun, dun!' But in a non-'ta-da' way.

FENLEY. I think that's the second part of *Eureka*.

O'CONNOR. Oh yeah, I remember that dance. I forget how *Hemispheres* ends—it ends in some kind of other way that makes you eat the continuum, it goes into your body somehow. And I remember thinking, 'Well, this isn't foxy—she's not being sly.' It doesn't have a ta-da factor. Somehow it was like clipping the continuum. There was something about it that was really successful.

FENLEY. Well, I think it's this idea that the continuum is happening before the dance begins and after it ends.

O'CONNOR. You're just bringing it into everything.

FENLEY. Yeah, and you're riding it that period of time. And when the wave is over, boom!—you're gone.

O'CONNOR. And then people can select to go back to real time or back to *that* time, in a way.

FENLEY. Right. It stops so that the idea can reverberate, I think. And it's in that reverberation that you're saying this artwork has happened. It has taken place over real time—you sat there and watched it, and now it's over. And what is its resonance? Is it moving you to do something yourself? Are you a better person because you witnessed it? Are you a worse person because you witnessed it? Does it have any effect? I think that reverberation is what we really need for artists to be working with.

O'CONNOR. One of the things I've been thinking of doing is to look at all the ways in my work that I could—what's the word?—take on the audience's point of view as a role and invite it into the process of making things. The idea that people leave the theatre and come to terms with what you've made is how I want to make my endings, so that the endings are in the process of boring into your neurology. So that it's not finished—it continues. You're going to be the final editor in your memory. So I don't want to do anything, taking from the history of dramatic structure that would make it . . .

FENLEY. . . . a finalization.

O'CONNOR. . . . the tyranny of drama, you know? Take that away and say, 'You and where you are in the world—where the world is—and your walking away from the theatre and forgetting this is going to make this piece finished. I'm going to create a wind that collects the stuff of the world and brings it before you.' And that's what I am working on now, and I feel like that's something that is going on in you as you work. I actually think that dance—if

IMAGE 23 *Eureka* (1982); Molissa Fenley in photo session in New York; costume by Yonson Pak. Photograph by Jack Mitchell © 1982.

people could be freed up to take it in—is, in a way, a much easier art form than a lot of people think.

FENLEY. Well, they are mystified by the whole deal!

O'CONNOR. Totally, I know.

FENLEY. I think abstract dance is the most beautiful thing to watch and to experience.

O'CONNOR. To go through.

FENLEY. Yeah. I just saw Merce [Cunningham]'s show the other night . . .

O'CONNOR. Me too.

FENLEY. . . . and the piece with the Rei Kawakubo costumes! It's just really extraordinarily beautiful.

O'CONNOR. It's glorious! And it really sculpts time. It's chopping up time for you in a way that is just so . . . glorious. And the music for that, too! God, it was extraordinary.

FENLEY. David Behrman's music.

O'CONNOR. Cunningham is really the place where I want to dress up in a nun's outfit and say, 'I want to try and help you! I like this!' Bring people to the light! It is an intense experience. Maybe there are just different types of people . . but I think there are filters that people have that don't allow them to get to what is so mystical about it all, you know?

FENLEY. Merce has a trajectory that is followed through each work. You know when it's going to end because suddenly all 15 people are back onstage. I mean, it almost always happens, and I find it so interesting and lovely, as a kind of nod-to-this-finalization onset at the end of the dance, yet . . .

O'CONNOR. . . . but then the curtain goes down and the dance is still going on.

FENLEY. And you know that it's a moment in time being stopped. That's just so great because, as I said, it's a nod to this need that we seem to have for a beginning, middle and an end. That's really brained into you from day one—that that is what you want.

O'CONNOR. It's a Western cultural idea.

FENLEY. Absolutely. That's another really wonderful thing about performing in Japan—that it is not the issue. Often the end is simply: another door opens and off you go someplace else. This thing of opening doors for people is a really important thing.

O'CONNOR. Yes, in any way that you can . . .

FENLEY. In any way. I think that the vocabulary in my work helps—that if you see the work over a period of time, that vocabulary becomes something that is signature and signifier. And that then, if you are seeing the work over a period of time, you get that, and then that takes you to another level too.

O'CONNOR. In fact, with many artists—and visual artists—you see a body of their work to see *one* thing, so it really does something to your understanding of it.

FENLEY. And that's something really missing in our culture—this idea of going to see a body of work. I mean, I have some critics who saw my work in the early 80s and have not come back. And it's like: 'Just think of your own life trajectory. What you did when you are 25 is not what you are doing when you are 50.' But this idea of making art as a lifetime pursuit—that's what we're doing. And there are periods in one's life, there are things that are interesting when you are older that are not when you are younger.

O'CONNOR. There are all these transitions . . .

FENLEY. Everyone is going through transitions!

O'CONNOR. I actually wanted to ask you that, because you've had a pretty anomalous journey here. You had such an enormous, unprecedented visibility in your early, early career. I've been talking about this recently—there are very few artists who are still going at something, as opposed to creating something that has their name on it and continuing to sell that thing. Like Merce, you, this woman Odile Duboc from France who I've just got turned onto—people that keep turning the corner and saying, 'What else?' But that's what I'm interested in doing. What do you feel about that? I know it's like that for everyone, but it's been quite an anomaly, your experience, I'd say. I can't think of anyone else that's had this thing.

FENLEY. Well, 30 years—2007 will be my thirtieth year.

O'CONNOR. That's a kind of continuum, how you've gone through it all.

FENLEY. It's gone through many, many ups and downs, the whole gamut—from working with a company at first, to working as a soloist with visual artists for 10 years, then back to a company. When you think about it, you're just living it, you're in it—and time passes. I remember when I decided to drop my company and work as a soloist—it was a year of discomfort with how things were going. I'd had a company for a number of years, Scottie and Silvia both left and other dancers replaced them. I had to teach them repertory and I felt like I was treading water—it was like, 'Let me out of here! I'm out!' I got out of it, and then suddenly all these other doors opened and I made *State of Darkness*, etc. So that was a whole reinvention of my self. Then one day, after doing all that, I started getting really lonely and thought that I should have a company again. And then I had that terrible accident. As far as many other people were concerned, that was the end of my career—they're still waking up to the fact that I'm still dancing.

O'CONNOR. That's a big issue.

FENLEY. Anyway, I got lonely and I got people again. And I love it!

O'CONNOR. It's almost like a dance—it starts out with some people and then leads with a solo, then you fall and come back in! It's like a really long dance.

FENLEY. I feel the same. I feel that everything is interconnected, that one thing leads to another. Also, to look back on older work, like reconstructing *Hemispheres*—to embody it not just on someone else but to make myself do it again. Oh man! I loved it! It was like being in someone else's dance company. I had to relearn stuff I hadn't done in years. And just relive that whole thing, and then here it is, years and years later, and I'm experiencing it with these other women who are half my age. I love that, because I'm dancing right in there with them!

O'CONNOR. Yeah, you are! That's like an old kind of discussion, because the way you are—and some other people are—it's not an issue that you're older than they are, it doesn't seem like a theme at all.

FENLEY. No, it doesn't seem like a theme to me. It just feels like it's very natural. I feel ultimately that I dance my work the best. It's that simple.

O'CONNOR. I actually think that's one of the things I want to say to you, that sometimes people's dancing is really crucial to their making, and sometimes I think that the fact that their dancing is crucial to their making is a problem. I don't see that with you—you're the motor for it.

FENLEY. Even more when I'm not dancing. Like when I was laid up. I made pieces on Peggy Baker and Peter Boal. I could still kind of get up and give them the idea but the idea of not doing it myself is not interesting to me. I like doing it.

O'CONNOR. That's true. That is important in your work.

FENLEY. I love doing it. I get anxious when I'm not involved. When I make a piece for a ballet company and I have to watch it instead of dance in it, well, that's hard. Because I know that as an ensemble dancer, my being in the ensemble, it's like it's a feed. But I don't feel like my dancers are constantly referring back to me as to how they should be doing it—it's just that it's a feed.

O'CONNOR. It's an energy thing.

FENLEY. Yeah, and I love that. And I get that from them, too.

O'CONNOR. And for the viewer it's a point of reference. I also feel like you don't make them try to do it like you.

FENLEY. That's right.

O'CONNOR. It's a thing, and three people are doing it in three different ways, which I adore. I'm really committed to that in my work, also. Everyone should do it completely differently.

FENLEY. I have a really wonderful rehearsal director, Judith Renlay, who comes in towards the end of a rehearsal period. She helps me pack it together, when the disparate things that are too disparate, you know . . . . But also to find a way so that each dancer does it according to their personal translation, and I really like that. Everyone dances in terms of their own training, in terms of their own interests.

O'CONNOR. And that mirrors the audience too, because it's a reinterpretation of something. Anyone who sees your work is not going to know, because there are no signifiers, really, that are denoted in any dance, so everyone's interpreting. And even in the room, the dancers are playing that role of audience. To let that slip seems really helpful for the audience members. It's like, 'Oh, they are doing that, too.' Not on a frontal level.

FENLEY. On a subconscious level. I think that this idea that is open-ended—everyone has their own experience—and as you say, it's clear that that is the issue, that it's meant to be that way, because we don't look the same.

O'CONNOR. It's really beautiful in terms of an open ideology of 'Wow, this system is so finite— what you're doing. It's so specific. At the same time, it's really open.' And it really is a metaphor for language too—the millions of different ways people can suddenly use language, use all the same structures and words within one language but have their own variation. No one is the standard. And so it has that . . .

FENLEY. It becomes conversational. It becomes a dialogue between the dancers as they dance and, consequently, a dialogue with the people who watch.

O'CONNOR. Just a couple of things. What do you feel now about teaching? You have an appointment at Mills College for half the year, and I'm interested because that's starting to happen to me too. What is that like, to coexist in some of those things in your life?

FENLEY. Well, I go one semester a year, which works because it's a four-month period that's quite intensive. I live on campus, and I work with mainly the Masters graduating class who are doing their thesis. I go to rehearsals in the evenings—it's real hands-on. I really like that. I find that talking about choreographing, seeing people when they are younger, helping them find their own voice, helping them filter through what is interesting to them, what's not, giving them a wide array of information . . . . My big thing is visual art—I know a lot about twentieth-century art. Many dancers have never even heard of Picasso, much less Malevich or Mondrian. I like to give a lot of information on Frank Gehry and Frank Lloyd Wright—get the dancers outside of the dance thing! Because they'll get that, they get that through their history, or they get it.

O'CONNOR. They get it, it's not that big. (*Laughs.*)

FENLEY. Well, yeah, that's the problem. they're too into that. They need to get a wider array of knowledge. And the Music Department there is fantastic. They have the contemporary wing in the Music Department—it just has amazing people coming through. It's a great resource.

O'CONNOR. And how does it affect your making? Or does it?

FENLEY. Well, when I'm there, I can't make a thing!

O'CONNOR. Is it time or . . .

FENLEY. I think it's time. I can reconfigure things. I can take a dance that was maybe made for three and make it for 20, and within that have a very creative, wonderful time reconfiguring. But as far as actually making new language—I find that I'm just stymied, lost. I'm a real hermit when it comes to working. Even before my dancers come into the studio I do a lot of the work alone, I always have. At Mills I don't have big blocks of time. I have some, but I find that I'll be in there trying to make something and I'm thinking, 'Oh, I have to grade that paper.' Then also, in the university, you get so involved in faculty meetings—they're endless! Watch out! You are just consumed. But, because of that, there's this boiling pot. I come back and it's like boom! I go into the studio and make three works back to back!

O'CONNOR. So you just have a back-up in your system and you spit 'em out.

FENLEY. It sort of works. Hopefully that'll be the case for a couple of years, because I just signed a contract for three more years!

O'CONNOR. Sometimes I find that my teaching, because I make them ask continually widening questions, it's really affected my work.

FENLEY. It does make you ask questions of yourself, because they're asking questions. Also, you think, 'OK, if I were looking at Robert Ryman's work right now . . .' We're doing that in my class, so I'm looking at it too.

O'CONNOR. Right, exactly, you're reconsidering it.

FENLEY. This is part of the boiling thing I'm talking about. These things are starting—

O'CONNOR. You're feeding yourself.

FENLEY. Absolutely. It's really interesting, because, when I leave there, not only do I have this wonderful relief of making work again but I also find that some corner has been turned. You were asking about how is this thing—the continuum—doing this for three years, and how to make new work. I think it's getting involved with other people that is helpful to turn constantly new pages.

I just made a piece, *Patterns and Expectations*, with Fred Frith music, a wonderful composer. Joan Jeanrenaud, the cellist, commissioned him to make the score for her and William Winant, who is a wonderful percussionist. Not only are the cello and percussion going, but there are moments where suddenly she plays the cello with a chopstick or Willie tears up a newspaper or throws a ping-pong ball or something is dropped on the floor. I thought it would be interesting if the dancers echoed those actions too—it's kind of Dada.

O'CONNOR. That's really interesting—take someone else's impulse and play with that.

FENLEY. Exactly. And we're having so much fun with it. That's actually the piece we're doing at the DUMBO festival.

O'CONNOR. That's interesting to me, because sometimes I look at what Merce does—he's just like, 'I'm going to do my dance, and you can put whatever you want on it.' Basically, it doesn't matter, it's unwreckable.

FENLEY. And all of that information that he gets from the computer—the body moving through space, the possibilities. It's changed the vocabulary so much—it's just opened it up.

That iPod thing was really funny. I liked the idea a lot, but . . . words, hearing a song . . .

O'CONNOR. Hearing words was really weird. And a regular, metred, quantized tempo was not what he's getting in there. It's a much more ragged musicality.

FENLEY. Still, what an experiment.

O'CONNOR. Totally interesting, of course. The basic metaphor of everyone being by themselves in the audience—you're having your own experience, and I'm just going to put spray paint on that and make you notice that. It's your own experience and it's communal. Of course he's just endlessly new, you know?

FENLEY. That's really filmic too—you go to a film . . . and I don't know about you, but I'd much rather watch a film with other people in a movie theatre than watch it on DVD.

O'CONNOR. But not with a friend. I like to go by myself—in a group of people, definitely . . .

FENLEY. . . . but among strangers, witnessing in a void. And there's something really fascinating . . .

O'CONNOR. . . . really compelling.

FENLEY. . . . about that. I think that's why live performance is so great. To be there . . .

O'CONNOR. . . . with everybody . . .

FENLEY. . . . and you're just like this thing in a sea. It's such a great, freeing thing. That's the other thing about art—let's free ourselves up.

O'CONNOR. That's totally what it does, yeah. For myself and for you people who have been doing this for a long time, I notice that the way I look at everything has been totally altered because I spent so much time making work. The way I look at everything. I hope that can happen for audiences sometimes. I think it can to different people at different degrees.

FENLEY. Right. When you're making work, you're inside your own head and that head is either engaged in the cultural world or it's not engaged in the cultural world.

O'CONNOR. And/or it's filtering it into its own cultural nature.

FENLEY. Well, what I mean by that is: there's this dialogue that goes on—you see it more in the visual arts—this idea of a dialogue that artists then feed into, sort of like a strain—maybe it's installation art or whatever. Then you have someone who is still painting over the edge—that person feels really isolated. But meanwhile that person is making explorations for herself/himself that's within a dialogue of painting throughout the time, the culture. I think what happens with marketing is that everything gets narrowed down to where the dialogue is between the last five years and the next five years. That's why it's so interesting for me to look at people like Malevich or Mondrian or Agnes Martin—their dialogue takes place over a very wide, expansive period of time. That continuum—getting back to that term, which is such a good one—is what I want to get into. I want a dialogue with those people!

O'CONNOR. It's so interesting to think about how I'm doing my work. Where I'm going in my work right now is less and less result-oriented. It's more about what am I doing in that room, or what are the inherent politics of my process. The product could keep getting just more and more what it is.

I've been seeing a lot of younger work, and there's some unstated rules in a lot of it, which are: no dancing, no finite ending (because that's bourgeois or something). There's a bunch of little things going on which I'm sorry about because I want people to go on their own journeys. I think contemporary art forms should open up and multiply and multiply and multiply the types of voices because to me the more it comes to a consensus, the more it is like our ugly friend's religion. And government.

FENLEY. It's just all about a narrowing down of the mind so you don't question it.

O'CONNOR. Yes, and I see it in a lot of younger work now, that it's looking back in itself. It's interesting, but there's a bunch of givens that are almost requirements, and I hope that people will crack that a little.

FENLEY. Is the anti-dance thing a rebellion against the period before them? Against Paul Taylor or something? I mean, what do you think that is?

O'CONNOR. I don't really know. I think that some of it is an affect, perhaps an erroneous look at what is a 'European' affect or . . . I don't know exactly, but some of it is anti-establishment of some sort. People come at it from different ends. I think a lot of people are interested in performance art.

FENLEY. When I was starting to choreograph, you wanted to go against Grand Union. You wanted to dance again! That was the thing. Johanna Boyce, and me and Charlie Moulton, and Bill T. Jones—we were all dancing.

O'CONNOR. Well, that's the thing that I wish would become contemporary. That all these forms that we've gone through—we've gone through Judson, the 80s, through Martha—that they all become part of a toolbox that can represent a different texture within one work. So you can go from something really conceptual to something representational to something commercial, and that becomes a reflection of a moment that's really advanced, just in terms of time moving forward in history. Not as in postmodernism, either. It's not referring to the source, it's just assuming it.

FENLEY. I think when people are young, though, it's helpful to have mandates that get you going. Because I remember when I was young—and I'm sure there are still people that are angry at me about it—you know . . .

O'CONNOR. What?! I'm sure I've got people angry at me, too! (*Both laugh.*)

FENLEY. But the point is when you are a young person you're sort of on a mission.

O'CONNOR. You have to be the generating step.

FENLEY. Yeah! And you have to be a little bit arrogant, because you have to settle yourself, you have to place yourself in this thing that you are a newcomer to. So you have to come in, head first.

O'CONNOR. Yeah, show 'em up!

FENLEY. And everyone gets angry, you know? And then you find, 25 years later, they're still angry!

O'CONNOR. Well, I love a lot of this work. I've been watching it. And now there's a bunch of reiterative elements, let's say, in people's work.

FENLEY. Like it's mannerist. That's the problem. If it's not on its own trajectory, it gets mannerist.

O'CONNOR. Definitely. And I mean, if the trajectory isn't like 'exit where you just were', basically lean forward, forward instead of going back. It's a really huge discussion but it's something that I look at. And what I see now is like 'Wow, I could do this, I could do this, I could do this.' Going back to these role model things, I want to go to Merce's every time and see him be in this other kind of examination again and again and again. Or I go to Pina, and I know what it is. She's never going to get rid of characters and just do one kick in repetition. It's not going to change, it's called Pina, and it's PINA.

So that's the thing that I am looking for in my life right now. There are very few role models for an older artist. If you are a visual artist, you would look at Matisse, who did paper-cuts at the end and summed it all up!

FENLEY. That's why I think as a choreographer there is a really wide world to look at through Matisse. There aren't necessarily role models in dance culture, because it's still so relatively new.

O'CONNOR. That's true. It's new—this phenomenon of people dancing time for a long time, and making for a long time, other than a couple of people. I think people are going into their fifties in a really different way than they used to. It will be interesting to see.

FENLEY. Well, yeah, into their fifties and still dancing . . . I mean, Trisha is still dancing, which is great.

O'CONNOR. I know! Oh my God, I saw her and she looked like she was 14!

FENLEY. Brilliant. And Merce danced until he was—even with a walker! It's so great.

It's really interesting to see—just talking about Merce again for a second. In that piece *Crises* from 1960, there are movements in there that were so particular to him, to what he does with men, because what he does with men is different from what he does with women, I think.

O'CONNOR. Yes.

FENLEY. There's this sort of balletic boxing thing that it was so interesting to see it early on—it's like it gets down . . .

O'CONNOR. . . . it gets grody and down low and punchy, very interesting. (*Laughs.*)

FENLEY. That's something that I've seen in many of the works . . .

O'CONNOR. It was really interesting to see that piece, and to see that that's where he came from. You can see both the seeds and the moment—the exit. You can see both the newness and what he was trying to get away from. Do you think there's any other stuff you want to cover while we're having this talk?

FENLEY. Well, we were talking about the sort of Zen concept, and I think that's a helpful thing to talk about. I think for a young person it's a very interesting thing to see. You and I have a very different . . . when we got here, it was not so expensive—I lived in a place for 15 dollars a month! I rented a room from some guy.

O'CONNOR. I had a house on Vestry Street for a hundred dollars a month—a loft.

FENLEY. I worked on Wall Street for a long time, I just punched in at 6 a.m., worked until two o'clock and then made dances the rest of the day.

O'CONNOR. With really cheap studios.

FENLEY. Absolutely. And I know people are not able to do that now. So there is a really different life force that these kids have when they're coming . . . And I think it's helpful for them to see that you can make it. That this life of making art—you have to Zen it!

O'CONNOR. You have to Zen it out! The really, really positive side of a lot of this work is that the work is the result of the situations. You know, making work in your house or . . .

FENLEY. Which is so interesting.

O'CONNOR. Totally. That's the thing that is really free and open and new about it. These people are—that's not rebellious, it's just the situation. They're not looking at the role model of 'single artist/company'—that's not even in their dreams! So it really unleashes up to this whole other thing that's really interesting to watch.

FENLEY. There are all these situations that have been happening before, and they can just cull from one to another. I mean, David Appel makes living-room dances . . .

O'CONNOR. I know David Appel's work!

FENLEY. I just think they're so interesting.

O'CONNOR. I wish we didn't have this grant situation where every year you have to produce something. There could be more space for these other voices for people who work in smaller ways or to see that whole range of things. Well, some people are doing that—in Brooklyn, there's places to see that stuff.

FENLEY. It's interesting doing these group shows. I just did one at the Flea the other night, and someone said to me, 'Oh, it's so brave of you to go back to working in such an alternative space!' Because the other people in the evening were like, you know, 13 years old! And I just said, 'Well, you know, I don't have a season this year—I'm working on a season for next year—but I just want to keep in the mix!' It's not an embarrassment to play in a small place—it's actually really fun! I had a great time. And Richard Move was in the Dance Conversations at the Flea—he was the moderator at the end—and it was a hoot to talk to him again. It's been a while. I think that work should get made, under any circumstances.

O'CONNOR. That's a really great point.

FENLEY. And just young kids have to know that! You just have to get out there and just every day get something made, or think about it, or do your research, or whatever.

O'CONNOR. I'm amazed at how many exciting people there are out there, doing it, in these conditions. I'm shocked, really.

FENLEY. And thank goodness for that! That they are making it!

O'CONNOR. Totally. There's a whole thing going on of young work that is very impressive. It's amazing. Well, I'm going to end this here, maybe we will have another conversation next year. But it was really nice talking to you.

FENLEY. Well, I timed it—it was exactly an hour.

O'CONNOR. It's like a TV show! (*Both laugh.*)

IMAGE 24, (facing page) **IMAGE 25** *Energizer* (1980); Molissa Fenley, Lynne Allard, Pat Graf, Susanna Weiss in performance at Dance Theater Workshop, New York; costumes by Yasha and Yonson Pak. Photograph by Paula Court © 1980.

Visual Dance

Paz Tanjuaquio

Molissa Fenley's dance is typically performed in a theatrical space, yet her choreography is less like 'theatre' than it is like viewing contemporary artworks in a gallery or museum, where ideas are conveyed through form and imagery. It is work most cogently experienced and its full visual complexity made visible through this lens of contemporary art—it is a visual dance in which we witness a composition of form and image emerge and develop over time.

I first came to know about Molissa's work through her collaborations with prominent contemporary visual artists. That first encounter happened in November 1989 at the Spreckels Theater in San Diego, where she performed her groundbreaking solo works *State of Darkness* to Igor Stravinsky's *Rite of Spring*, and *The Floor Dances: Requiem for the Living* to music by Henryk M. Gorecki, with a sculptural installation by Richard Long. It was Long's work that enticed me to see the show. At the time, I saw myself primarily as a visual artist working at the Museum of Contemporary Art San Diego (known then as the La Jolla Museum of Contemporary Art) where I had also been involved with the installation of Long's earthworks. For Molissa's dance, Long's stones formed a wide circle centrestage where Molissa performed her solo entirely on the floor, inserting ever-shifting movement among the large rocks. Described as a response to the devastation of wild life caused by the Alaska oil spill earlier that year, the solo, as the *New York Times*' Anna Kisselgoff said, was 'completely original, using a crescendo of movement attached to the floor with invention and feeling. The wounded bird here is also the shaman who can enter the world of the animal spirits' (1988: n.p.). I found an immediate affinity with the work, not only because I had just created an abstract painting in response to the Exxon Valdez oil spill, a triptych of a deep-sea blue blending into black, but also because I saw, for the first time, the possibilities of integrating dance and visual arts into transformative performance art.

Since that encounter, I have associated Molissa's dances with the visual arts and find in her choreography the intellectual rigour and complex patterning that you might see in abstract painting, right down to titles that give reference to the work's inspiration. With a palette of propulsive phrasing, distinct design of space and movement derived from her sculpted body, Molissa creates the illusion of expansive terrain and designs environments that call for contemplation and invite the viewer on a journey. For both the dancer and the viewer, her performances can elicit an emotional response reached through sheer physicality and that mirrors the subtle yet enlightening transformation one goes through after a long hike or the inspiration from watching a runner complete a marathon. Yet, beyond the physical, there is a poetic resonance in viewing her performances.

Years later, I would be dancing Molissa's dances and intimately come to know her process.

The Path to Dance

Before I met Molissa, I was a visual artist. I studied at the University of California San Diego and was immersed in a theoretical approach that emphasized idea-making and encouraged the exploration of diverse artistic forms. We studied directly with influential artists like Manny Farber and performance spectacle with Happenings originator, former painter Allan Kaprow. But I discovered I needed physicality to explore ideas; so I ventured into modern dance and was introduced to New York choreographers such as Ron Brown and the late Woody McGriff, experiences that, along with Molissa's concert, helped me to gravitate towards dance. Movement ultimately became my medium, and, years after attending New York University's Tisch School of the Arts and receiving an MFA in dance, I saw a residency opportunity to work with Molissa as a master artist at the Atlantic Center for the Arts in New Smyrna Beach, Florida. I grabbed it, and it was then that I first met Molissa.

During the three-week residency, I got to take her daily technique class and to learn the first part of her work *Sita*. Soon after, Molissa invited me to perform the complete solo *Sita* at the Joyce Theater in late January and early February 1997. The concert was structured around three solos, two of which were danced in alternation by guest artists: Molissa premiered *Trace*, which she alone performed; she and I danced *Sita* on alternate nights; and I shared *Pola'a* with Peter Boal, then a dancer with New York City Ballet. Originally I was scheduled to perform Thursday, Saturday and Sunday nights, but, just before the show opened, Molissa decided to have me perform *Sita* opening night in her place. I was honoured. I was also prepared, and elated to be in the opening piece on the programme. The 20-minute solo set in four sections was a landscape through time, a dance that travelled through ever-widening spaces that David Moodey's lighting made visible. There were spatial landmarks for the dance as it progressed, the lighting expanding on the floor as the choreography progressed. Projected onstage were black-and-white photos by Sandi Fellman depicting the close-up contours of a dancer's body, a blurred landscape of shape and form. The challenge in dancing the solo was not yielding to the beauty of the music, set to Etudes for Piano by composer Philip Glass, performed live by Martin Goldray. Preparing for the solo, I often would imagine viewing the dance as the audience, seeing myself in a deep bright-red velvet costume against the grey scale of the backdrop. I realize now that it was a way of visualizing the dance, and it was a mechanism I would continually use in learning Molissa's complex movement.

Sita and the other works I would come to perform meant that I began to delve into Molissa's training which is dependent on endurance, strong technique and physical clarity. Everything is precisely choreographed. She would teach us the intricate movement, demonstrating a phrase a few times and moving on to show more material. To remember them, we dancers would often write down the myriad phrases that we had just learnt, each phrase named in relation to its sequential number or by the specific steps involved. Often these phrases were reordered, juxtaposed or repeated, each module of movement becoming a recognizable visual pattern. From her earlier works to more recent pieces, you as a dancer not only have to learn the movement quickly but also be able to know it so well that you can reorder the phrases as she chooses. This was the case with the 2004 revival of *Hemispheres* at the Kitchen, with music by Anthony Davis performed by a 10-piece avant-garde jazz band. It was exhilarating to have interaction with live music that seemed timeless and new each time and that mirrored the spontaneity of Molissa's distinctive movement. But this was also a rhythmically complex work, with many changes of metre. We had to learn phrases of 35 fives or 7-3s, and count 10s against 11s, which was a challenge of time and endurance. But all the dances I have performed—*'Ice, Dew, Food, Crew, Ape'*; *Delta*; *331 Steps*; *Lava Field*; *On the Other Ocean*; *Escalay*; *Short Stories*; *Sky Garden*; *Water Courses*; *Kuro Shio*; and, most recently, *Credo in Us*—have presented a particular set of metrical, spatial, intellectual and emotional challenges.

Visualizing the Dance

In learning Molissa's choreography, the dancer has to fully embody the nuances of the movement. Particularly important is initiating movement from the back so that the arms extend from the spine and lengthen through the fingertips. Hands, like blades, have to press through the air, which gives the movement its tensile shape and sculptural definition. To create an expansive quality, the dancer's gaze must draw the focus out as if seeing into the distance. With gestural material, like *Lava Field*, nothing is ever improvised. Nor is there ever any discussion of how a dancer should feel. This is not to suggest that Molissa's dances are devoid of feeling; it simply means that the act of dancing in the moment is the conduit for impact on the performer and the viewer. This is where Molissa's approach is most like the visual arts and parallels how paint or other materials have no emotion until the hand guides it into a form. One goes into the rehearsal space as a painter or writer goes into a studio. One is also the material, and Molissa begins to form us with a regimen of hour-long warm-ups, an aspect of discipline that resonates in and supports the stamina demanded by her choreography. It also shapes our physicality and stays long after. We learn phrases seemingly drawn in indelible ink—there is no retouching or changes made once the movement has been learnt and set.

Dancing with Molissa through these years, I have found her generous and encouraging as a mentor. I have continued creating my own works and on several occasions she has invited me to present my choreography in her programmes, such as a collaboration with composer Todd Richmond, *Twelve*, in 2000 during her *Three Evenings of Dance* at Joyce Soho, and a duet *The Divide* (2010) at the 92Y Harkness Dance Festival during *Molissa Fenley and Friends*. In 2008, I asked Molissa to create a solo for me based on *Soundless Music*, a 1952 unpublished manuscript by Yoko Ono. I gave her Ono's text and she set it to John Cage's silent score *4′33″*. After reading the manuscript, she found several items in the rehearsal space at my Topaz Arts studio that became modified parts of the piece, notably, a long bamboo pole and a wooden ladder-like structure—picking up and moving the props as if performing a task rather than a dance and finding a relationship with the object as if it were almost like another dancer. The pole came next, and several images emerged for me in performing it—at times it felt like a balancing pole, or carrying tool, an oar or just a rod that, in the end, of the 4 minutes and 33 seconds, I lie beside and rest my foot against. A transformation takes place as an intimate relationship is developed with the objects. Eventually the 10-foot white pole, designed by artist Todd Richmond, became part of Molissa's later solo *Mass Balance*, part of a 2010 series called *The Prop Dances*, for which she invited artists to create a central visual and interactive element for her dances.

To see Molissa collaborate again with visual artists is to witness a cyclic return to the kind of deeply influential work of hers I first encountered. Visual elements are never mere props or backdrops for her work but are entwined physically, spatially and conceptually in the process, capturing all at once the physicality, form and intellectual thought of the dance so that dance and visuals arts become integrated as one memorable and mesmerizing experience. I treasure the moments when Molissa shares a brand-new piece—performing it in a rehearsal studio to me is at its most powerful, the way viewing artwork in a gallery is, or visiting an artist's studio and seeing where the work is created. The generosity she brings out while performing makes you aware that you are experiencing a work of art in the act of being made. Her daily regimen informs her body and in watching her dances, the audience watches a dancer in command of her form—truly embodying 'live art'.

Works Cited

KISSELGOFF, Anna. 1988. 'In "State of Darkness", a Dancer's Rite of Passage'. *New York Times*, 8 October. Available at: www.nytimes. com/1988/10/08/-arts/review-dance-in-state-of-darkness-a-dancer-s-rite-of-passage.html (last accessed on 5 February 2015).

IMAGE 26 *Entrance* (2014); Molissa Fenley, Christiana Axelsen in performance at the Flea, New York. Photograph by Julie Lemberger © 2014.

IMAGE 27 *Dance an Impossible Space* (2014); Molissa Fenley, Rebecca Chaleff in performance at Judson Memorial Church, New York. Photograph by Julie Lemberger © 2014.

The Chair, and Other Pieces

David Moodey

The Chair

In 1995, Molissa blew out her knee. It was bad. We had just began a company run at the Joyce Theater in New York City, and on opening night she went down in a heap. The curtain dropped, and she was off to the hospital and soon into surgery. Although for a dancer it couldn't have been much worse, and I figured the knee blow-out was going to hold her down for quite some time, I never really thought it was the end for Molissa. This was Molissa Fenley. She had too much drive. I was optimistic.

Still, it was a complete surprise when she called after a couple of months and asked me to come into rehearsal and see the piece she was working on. I thought to myself, 'OK, I can see her back in the studio, moving cautiously, doing physical therapy, but actually *choreographing* a piece?' Because of my experience as her lighting designer, I knew the way she worked. She always had 75 per cent of the dance done before she called me in for an early viewing. Most of the broad strokes of the work would be in place, if not more. I wondered how, given the timing of her injury, she could be at such a place. It would mean she had begun choreographing a new work within four or five weeks of surgery. Given that she had torn the anterior cruciate ligament—the *x* band that holds the knee in place—and given the extent of the surgery, I knew Molissa still had to be on crutches.

I arrived with great curiosity at what was still the Dia Art Foundation rehearsal space. I walked up to the top floor, Molissa's favourite rehearsal room, puzzled by how she was making the trek to the space up the four long flights of stairs, curious about what I might find. Dance on crutches? In the middle of the room sat a lone chair. There was Molissa making her way around, as I had suspected, on crutches. I took my usual seat in front of the mirrors and looked at her.

'OK, what's up?' Molissa smiled, set the crutches aside, and sat in a chair in the centre of the studio. She asked me to start the music.

What I saw that afternoon was nothing short of brilliant.

Molissa sat in the chair and she danced on it and from it. It was a beautiful piece—graceful, imaginative and striking. She moved in ways I couldn't have imagined and pushed herself into a new physical language based upon the chair in the middle of open space. The piece, at least 10 to 12 minutes long, at no point seemed a dance of confinement or limitation. In fact, her injury seemed of almost no consequence. This was so true that if the audience knew nothing about her injury, they would have had a hard time gleaning from the performance that there was an injury and that that injury placed her there, in that chair. Molissa's inspiration was to move and choreograph, and as long as she had space and time to move through, she could not be held down or kept motionless.

The Chair Dance begins slowly, and I can see how she used it as a way to keep as much of her body in shape as possible and to keep her ever-active mind placated by new creation. I can still see her, on that first day, in that chair, in that rehearsal room. We were not talking about recovery, when we might work together again, about the pain or the limitations; we were talking about a piece, a new work, how to light it. We were right back in the thick of it, and not much more than a heartbeat had gone by. It amazed me for days, weeks; it amazes me still.

I was so moved by the experience that I designed the piece around that rehearsal room and around that day. The room had a skylight; the sun passed from east to west in the course of our afternoon together and that became the basis of my design. I wanted the audience to implicitly share the experience of how moved I was to see this elegant dancer throw aside all hindrance and get back to work. Back to her calling. Even now, long after her knee has healed, to see her perform the dance is to witness her valiant purpose.

Mr Pink Shirt

One of my earliest experiences with Molissa was going with the company to Japan as lighting director. The lighting designs were by Gary Mintz, a great mentor of mine, and I was determined to do well by him and the company. But I was green on all counts—at touring, at executing someone else's designs and at dealing with producers. To complicate matters, we were working in a space that was more like a high-school auditorium than a theatre. The performance space was very wide, not very deep and most of the stage and available dance space was on the apron. It required some real modifications to the original designs. Since I was green, I dutifully ran everything by Molissa. Spacing and such vital details as where the first piece began and where we were to be in the second piece and when we hit the special—all were to be reviewed together. So much of the design had to be worked out through trial and error, and we couldn't know the answers until we groped our way to them.

In those days the Molissa Fenley company took one tech person. That person—I, in this case—would oversee the load-in and set-up, would focus and cue the show, would stage manage the performance and act as company manager, would deal with the producers. If I was the go-to guy, my immediate contact, the guy in charge of the Japanese crew, was 'the man'. He presented and carried himself as 'the man', yet, in what seemed in direct conflict with his persona, he wore pink shirts. Mr Pink Shirt became my early window into the complex worlds one meets on tour.

Mr Pink Shirt had questions for me every five minutes: Where do you want this special? Where will the dancers be at the beginning of each piece? Where do the monitors go? Where do we hang the backlight? With each question, I would trot off and confer with Molissa. We'd discuss it, try something if necessary, and then I would get back to Mr Pink Shirt. Each time I returned with an answer, Mr Pink Shirt's irritation with me increased. It took me a while to figure out what Molissa already had.

Finally, Mr Pink Shirt made it quite clear to me: 'It's nice that you appease the woman, but we know who the decision makers are here: the men.' I was shocked. What did he mean? He was going to override Molissa's decision because she was a woman? I was flabbergasted as well as stymied. But Molissa was smart. She quickly assessed this guy and the situation and began to make choices that created the least conflict. She compromised when she could. She was discreet, and she often made it appear as though I had made the decisions. When necessary, she instructed me to tell Mr Pink Shirt that, as the designer, I wanted it this way or that. This is how I disarmed him. Mr Pink Shirt was placated.

Looking back on that trip, I realize how much Molissa taught me. I discovered how one goes about putting on the best show one can, which means to work within the given structures, regardless of whether you are in an opera house or a shoebox. Irrespective of the conditions, the goal of excellence is always the same. While Mr Pink Shirt should never be allowed to compromise your art, conflict and power struggles are real, and knowing how to manage them are essential to reaching the goal. While I have had plenty of disagreements with producers since that date in Japan, that early lesson in diplomacy has saved me from many unnecessary battles.

No Power (Italy)

As anyone who has toured knows, theatre spaces are vastly different both in how they are equipped and the way they are run. There is nothing ideal about having the new with the old in a theatre, and this is what we encountered on one of our trips to Italy. In 1987, Molissa and her dancers went to Florence, where the past and the present were at odds with each other. The theatre was in fact a wing of a large old villa, a glassed-in space known as an *orangeria*, the room that had once stored the villa's fruit trees for the winter, saving them from frost. This winter garden house was three times as long as it was wide, which made for an extensive performance space, and all new equipment had been installed, including new dimmers and circuit breakers. The power distribution throughout the theatre was beautiful. But the power to the theatre had never been upgraded. It came from a pole outside the building to a breaker box on the outer wall, farthest from the control station where we ran the lights and sound. Despite the new electrical equipment, it was still possible to run too many dimmers at the same time and blow the breaker on that far-far-away end of the building.

For this run, Molissa was performing *State of Darkness*, a beautiful and difficult piece set to Igor Stravinsky's *Rite of Spring*. Fiercely, she used all 33 minutes of the music and danced the piece topless, pushing boundaries in all directions. I was running the lighting board myself, and a few times during rehearsal runs I blew the breaker to the entire building and had to make a 100-yard walk to the opposite end of the space and reset the breaker, then return. On opening night, five minutes into a 33-minute piece we heard *POP*! and the entire theatre went black. There were no lights and no sound. In six seconds, I was down the stairs from the booth and running the 100-yard dash to the breaker box. Having been a sprinter in high school, I reached it in good time, but it occurred to me, on the return sprint, that with the throwing of the breaker, all the lights would come back on but the sound would not restart until the button was pushed. I begin to shout, 'Start the sound, start the sound,' for, just as I suspected, Molissa was frozen in the exact position she had been when the lights went out.

She did not drop character, did not begin explaining the problem to the audience, she stood ready to resume. It had to be a good 15 to 20 seconds in the dark and another 15 to 20 seconds in the light with no sound. Seconds seem like minutes in situations like these. But when the sound resumed, so did she, without a hitch, dancing on for another 28 minutes as though nothing had gone wrong. The audience loved it, loved her. And I had to marvel at the concentration, the focus and sheer strength on her part.

The Rocks

Molissa has always looked for ways to broaden her boundaries. And she often sought out other groundbreaking artists to work with—musicians, painters, sculptors—a vast array of collaborators to engage in the creative process. One of them was the sculptor Richard Long. For Molissa's newest piece at the time, *Nullabor*, he built a beautiful rock array. The collection of stones formed a band about 10 feet in width, leaving a 20-foot-diameter void in the middle, and this was the performance space, making the whole about 40 feet across. It was a feat to get the rocks delivered, unloaded and dispersed in a Manhattan theatre according to the artist's plan. They were solid granite, and there were over 375 stones. The granite was extremely heavy, and it needed many a large crew for set up. I had to customize the lighting, meanwhile, in order to accentuate the sculpture in relation to the dance.

Despite the effort, the payoff was huge. The choreography was stunning. Molissa never left the confines of the inner circle and never lost our attention for a second. She was a salmon swimming upstream, a seagull trapped in an oil spill—she was everything your imagination could conjure up. She related to the rocks, and she had specific ones that had to be in a specific place for a specific moment in the piece. It was mesmerizing and blended the two art forms beautifully. It was one of those works that had to tour. But shipping 375 granite rocks around the world was totally impractical; an adapted version had to be invented to take on the road. Molissa decided that a single array of rocks in a circle 20 feet in diameter would do, but they still had to be granite of the same size and proportion as the originals. This became one of the funnier bits of touring in our many years together. We would arrive in, say, Italy, and on the first day of load-in, I would begin set-up in the theatre while Molissa and the local producer sought out a nearby quarry to hunt down the perfect rocks. People often thought it strange that it couldn't be just any rocks; we couldn't just have a few people run out to Home Depot or its Italian equivalent. In fact, Molissa had to be there to select the rocks—they had to be the right size and shape—and then she and I would arrange and re-arrange them until we had the best facsimile of the original. With time, we could do it in rep with other pieces, because we designed a numbering system so the rocks could go back in the same place each time. She was the consummate professional and perfectionist.

No Music

This piece amazed me every time. And it was my watching it over and over that made me understand how remarkable it was. The piece was almost 20 minutes long. It was done in complete silence and was like magic to me as I sat in the wings, calling the cues. Without music or sound of any kind all the cues were taken from the movement. As I have mentioned before, Molissa is a perfectionist in every good sense. Pieces were not built to be performed later in a loose facsimile of the original; they were to be performed the way they were originally choreographed. This piece was a shinning example of that dedication. No one in the audience could ever truly know the extent of her professionalism when it came to this piece; you would have to watch and time the piece, as I did, on many occasions. Of the countless times Molissa danced this piece, she was always, without fail, within 10 seconds of the original timing. It was uncanny to me, how she could maintain the speed of each movement, keep the spacing and the distance and hence the timing so exact despite the change in venues. Big theatres, little theatres, long and narrow, short and deep—it didn't matter—she would stick within 10 seconds of her ideal. It was astounding, really. Try doing something for just three minutes at exactly the same speed every time. Dang, that's hard. And 19 minutes, not varying, plus or minus 10 seconds? This is a testament to Molissa's deep focus and unerring sense of time in space within her body. She rehearsed this work until without any landmarks from the external world, music or otherwise, she could capture that precision every time. The silence grew on you—it began as a gentle breeze you were just barely aware of, then that breeze intensified and brought itself to your immediate consciousness. It made you revel in the fact that this was pure dance—nothing else, just dance. The breeze refreshed you and you rode along with it. Each movement, each phrase could be fully explored and enjoyed for itself—not for how it related to the score, the scenery, the lighting, but for how it related to itself. Just the dance. As a result, she etched this piece in my memory for ever.

As I reflect on these stories, I realize they are mostly about Molissa's strength of character. Some people call it passion, others conviction. Whatever label one uses, Molissa has it. She brings it to every theatre, rehearsal hall or meeting. It's part of her soul. We see it in all aspects of her life. She is just as fervent helping a fellow artist through a difficult time, and is the first to volunteer for a benefit concert, or say yes to a show that will only bring in enough money to pay the dancers. This spirit is most evident in her work. The reach for perfection is in every move of every rehearsal or performance. Even though she knows that perfection is very rarely achieved, I have never once seen her strive for anything less.

IMAGES 28, (facing page) **IMAGE 29** *Mix* (1979); Kate McLaughlin, Elizabeth Streb, Molissa Fenley, John Bernd in performance at the Kitchen, New York. Photograph by Lois Greenfield © 1979.

Mix

Elizabeth Streb

In 1978, the choreographer Neil Greenberg introduced me to Molissa Fenley. She and I were both young, and that year I began rehearsals with her on a dance called *Mix* which was to be presented at the Kitchen, curated by Eric Bogosian. I was one of four dancers that included Molissa. On the initial day of rehearsal, as I walked in the door, she asked, 'How old are you?' I said, '28!' She said, 'I'm 23!' about five years younger than me.

As we started learning *Mix*, I discovered the structure was geometric and, as time went on, it unfolded and unfurled in mysterious ways. That first day, Molissa began teaching the steps in lanes. She relied on many sketches, which were beautiful and colour-coded—the maps, the rules of the road of the dance that we would trace as we learnt the piece. Each pass across the lane would be a series of locomotive steps that involved torso and arm movements intricately and rhythmically connected to what was happening in the legs and served to take us across the room. I was a very fast learner and I liked the dance right away.

Eventually *Mix* grew to be 50 minutes of non-stop rhythmic variations on a percussive theme with a beat and a timing system that only Molissa fully understood. It felt organic and fundamental, as if it came from a long, long time ago, when physical rhythms were not only embodied more deeply but were the essence of what there was to know. We carried sticks with us and beat them every so often, although I can't remember if these clangers made it into the final production.

Although I was not a 'counter'—a dancer who figures out the timing and then works to the beats—clearly *Mix* was carefully constructed along a line composed of moments that had varying durations, as well as pathways, directions, facings and distances. Since I was prone to memorize movement physically, when Molissa asked that we go to the eighteenth measure of the fifth variation, I had no idea where in the piece that section was! She said, 'You can't possibly do this without counting—please start counting.' And I remember trying very hard to count and getting lost, although I could easily tell, given the location of the other three people, where I was meant to be. Every so often she would say to me, 'Are you counting now, Elizabeth?' And I would answer, 'Of course I am, Molissa.' I hoped she couldn't tell one way or another at that point, since by then I had my own system for knowing where I was in time and place.

As we worked, it felt as if Molissa had us weaving a gorgeous Indian carpet pattern into and out from the centre of the space we were occupying. It took on talismanic qualities as we twisted, turned and stamped on constant diagonal crossings and meetings—an ecstatic quartet. At the time, Molissa was sometimes cited as an artist who might have been the offspring of Lucinda Childs and Laura Dean. Her propulsive and relentless locomotion pieces set to loud music seemed to become the air around us, its molecules, with its essence lording over the area we occupied. She appeared as if the movement was bursting out from her body without her permission, just streaming out, before the idea of streaming was coined for the Internet. Her work was 4-D in 3-D, and the physical 'doing' of it was transcendent. It started and lifted the spirit of us movers: up, up, up—slightly above the level of the ground. Sometimes it felt that we were changing everything as we spun rapidly and flailed our arms and heads.

I remember we were given very brightly coloured taffeta tops and bottoms to wear for the shows. On opening night, the very first move was an intensely powerful stamp and included a big curve of the entire torso so that the head and face kissed the knees. Immediately, the pants of my costume ripped across the back of my butt, and I still had about 45 minutes of the dance left to perform. I remember making the decision to, well, ignore it. What else could I do? The very next night, I had to decide to not hold back with my movements just because of my 'ripping' experience the night before. So out I went, and 'rrrrippppppp' again, this time it was my taffeta top, all across my chest . . . I made the same decision: Keep on with it. I believed that once a dancer began a Molissa Fenley dance, there was nothing left to do but finish. It would have been sacrilegious to stop or pause, especially for something so trivial as a set of clothes.

The third night, nothing tore.

IMAGE 30 *Ocean Walk* (*Regions*) (1995, revival 2010), Molissa Fenley in performance at Joyce Soho, New York; set by Roy Fowler. Photograph by Julie Lemberger © 2010.

Dance and the Nature of Mind

Rande Brown

In the summer of 1983, Shozo Tsurumoto asked me to help curate a festival of emerging American artists for the LaForet Museum and Performance Spaces in Tokyo. I had recently returned to New York from Japan, where I had studied Buddhist meditation and philosophy for over 10 years and had been active in what are loosely termed the Zen arts. I knew almost nothing about what was going on in the New York art world of the early 80s, but Tsurumoto knew I was interested in work that dealt with consciousness and asked me to orient my search in that direction.

I soon realized that three of the artists who were garnering the most attention at the moment not only happened to be dealing with the intersection of art and consciousness but were also women: Laurie Anderson, Molissa Fenley and Cindy Sherman. Their names cropped up constantly in discussions with visual and performance art curators. I went to see their work. Upon reflection, it seems now that all three were in the process of somehow capturing a historical moment, a point in time when raw feminism was evolving and beginning to inform a new, intelligent, thoughtful and compassionate voice for female artists. These three women were all actively trying to express the truth by examining the differences between the way things were and the way that they appeared. I proposed a festival of women artists, and Tsurumoto asked me to explore the possibility of bringing all three women to Tokyo. I found a contact for Molissa and set up a date for studio visit.

Molissa was working at a loft on North Moore Street, and I remember hiking up the stairs on a hot and sultry summer afternoon to enter a space that was open and cool. I was immediately impressed by Molissa's clarity, intelligence and vitality. Then I settled in to watch a rehearsal and was profoundly struck by what I saw. To my relatively untutored eye, it felt like Molissa was actually dancing the structure, the architecture, of consciousness. It was as if she was dancing the tension between clarity and delusion, between constraint and freedom. Years of friendship have only reinforced my initial response to the beauty of her work.

We invited Molissa to perform in Tokyo under the umbrella of The Next Wave of American Women festival and she graciously agreed. Molissa Fenley and Dancers performed *Hemispheres* at Laforet Harajuku from 28 April to 1 May 1984. The performances were met with great critical and popular acclaim. It is not surprising to me that the Japanese have been so supportive of Molissa's work over the ensuing years, because the pristine elegance of her lines, the quiet emotional power of her vocabulary and the essential purity of her artistic quest naturally and intensely resonate with the deeply held aesthetic principles of the Japanese soul. Her work is minimal but not bare. Like a perfect flower arrangement or an ink-brushed landscape, volumes of complex content shimmer within the spare lines of her images.

It has been my pleasure and privilege to witness the evolution of Molissa's work, her courageous explorations into the nature of movement, awareness and insight.

Epilogue: The Composite View

Stephen Greco

The view we have of existence is unavoidably our own, whether the context is home and dailyness or the universe and life itself. Much as scientists and philosophers have pondered the limits of subjectivism and anthropocentricity, they can't suggest a way beyond them. If we're lucky, we can use something like art to discern the qualities of our own attention and the limits of awareness.

It's a notoriously limited thing, awareness. There is *here*—the reality of my mind at this moment (which can be explored for ever, of course); and then there are several billion other *heres* that are just as real, for others. In embracing this multiplicitous view of existence, Molissa Fenley's work is more 'existential' than the showier, more thematically philosophical artwork that's often described that way, most of which holds that life is kind of dreary. Fenley's existentialism is nicer; her work is buoyant even when dark, absorbing in an invigorating way, and sometimes even fun to watch, in the sense of entertainment. And it brings you somewhere, if you let it—to a mental space that's as different from dully Sartrean, post–Second World War shell shock as a meditation is from a coma.

Each moment of Fenley's work seems to bring exhilarating news of uncharted depths, unmappable reaches—like the moments of consciousness that gurus say are the entry points to infinity. Fenley's infinity is not that of integers, though, but of the space between any two consecutive integers in which the choreographer discovers a thrillingly varied range of textures, dynamics and, if you will, conditions—just like Robert Ryman does in his white paintings and Mark Rothko in his black ones. In this way, Fenley's work is about *our* time, when modes of attention are simultaneously being fragmented and unified, and the panoptic gaze of the cellphone camera dwarfs anything that institutional surveillance ever proposed. The work can be thought of not only as academically 'postmodern' but simply, freshly modern—the way the brave, early modern artists thought of their work at the beginning of the last century, when everything, including looking and thinking, needed rethinking too.

Fenley rethinks, then makes absorbing compositions for space and time as it exists today—when there are almost seven billion other *heres*, thick with new bodies, new intentions, new momenta. Maybe that's why a set of diverse writings about Fenley makes such a great companion to her body of work. Even strong memories of great dance become more accurate when put side by side—in conversation, in writing—with other strong memories, for a composite view . . .

IMAGE 32, (facing page) IMAGE 33 *Planes in Air* (*The Prop Dances*) (2010); Molissa Fenley, Cassie Mey, Katie McGreevy in performance at Joyce Soho, New York; props by Roy Fowler. Photographs by Julie Lemberger © 2010.

IMAGE 31 *Pieces of Land* (*The Prop Dances*) (2010); Cassie Mey, Molissa Fenley in performance at Joyce Soho, New York; props by Jene Highstein. Photograph by Julie Lemberger © 2010.

Notes on Contributors

Philip Glass has had an extraordinary and unprecedented impact upon the musical and intellectual life of his times through his operas, his symphonies, his compositions for his own ensemble, and his wide-ranging collaborations with artists ranging from Twyla Tharp to Allen Ginsberg, Woody Allen to David Bowie. The operas—*Einstein on the Beach*, *Satyagraha*, *Akhnaten* and *The Voyage*, among many others—play throughout the world's leading houses. Glass has written music for experimental theatre and for Academy Award–winning motion pictures such as *The Hours* and *Kundun*, and *Koyaanisqatsi*, his initial filmic landscape with Godfrey Reggio and the Philip Glass Ensemble. His associations, personal and professional, with leading rock, pop and world music artists date back to the 1960s, including the beginning of his collaborative relationship with artist Robert Wilson. Glass is the first composer to win a wide, multi-generational audience simultaneously in the opera house, the concert hall, the dance world, in film and in popular music.

Bill T. Jones, artistic director, co-founder and choreographer at Bill T. Jones/Arnie Zane Dance Company, and artistic director of New York Live Arts, is the recipient of the 2014 Doris Duke Artist Award; the 2013 National Medal of Arts; the 2010 Kennedy Center Honors; a 2010 Tony Award for Best Choreography for *FELA!*; a 2007 Tony Award, 2007 Obie Award, and 2006 CALLAWAY Award for *Spring Awakening*; the 2010 Jacob's Pillow Dance Award; the 2007 USA Eileen Harris Norton Fellowship; the 2006 Lucille Lortel Award for Outstanding Choreography for *The Seven*; the 2005 Wexner Prize; the 2005 Samuel H. Scripps American Dance Festival Award for Lifetime Achievement; the 2005 Harlem Renaissance Award; the 2003 Dorothy and Lillian Gish Prize; and the 1994 MacArthur Genius Award. In 2010, Jones was recognized as Officier de l'Ordre des Arts et des Lettres by the French government, and in 2000, the Dance Heritage Coalition named him 'An Irreplaceable Dance Treasure'. He has created more than 140 works for his company.

Ann Murphy is assistant professor and chair of the Mills College Dance Department. As a dance critic for more than two decades, she has written for publications ranging from the *New York Times* and *Dance Magazine* to the *San Francisco Chronicle* and the Bay Area Newspaper Group. She is a contributor to *The Oxford Handbook of Screendance Studies* and to the monograph *Nework of Pointes*, while her essay 'Lucas Hoving and Jose Limon: Radical Dancers' has appeared in the collection *Jose Limon: The Artist Re-viewed*. In addition, she founded the Bay Area monthly publication *In Dance* and has been on the dance faculty at Mills College, Oakland, California for eight years.

Peter Boal, artistic director of Pacific Northwest Ballet, was raised in Bedford, New York. At the age of nine, after having seen a New York City Ballet performance of George Balanchine's *Coppélia*, he began studying ballet at the School of American Ballet, the official school of New York City Ballet. Boal became a member of New York City Ballet's corps de ballet in 1983, a soloist in 1987 and a principal dancer in 1989. In 2005, he retired from New York City Ballet after a 22-year career with the company. Boal was also a full-time faculty member at the School of American Ballet from 1997 to 2005. In 2003, he founded Peter Boal and Company, a critically acclaimed chamber ensemble. In 2005, upon his retirement from New York City Ballet, Boal became artistic director of Pacific Northwest Ballet and director of Pacific Northwest Ballet School.

Molissa Fenley was born in 1954, grew up in Ibadan, Nigeria, and returned to the United States in 1971. After graduating from Mills College in Oakland, California, she moved to New York City in 1975 and founded Molissa Fenley and Company in 1977. She has since created over 80 dance works—both group dances and solos made in collaboration with visual artists and contemporary composers. Her work has been presented throughout the United States, South America, Europe, Australia, India, Indonesia, Japan, Singapore, Korea, Taiwan and Hong Kong. Molissa is a Guggenheim Fellow, a Fellow of the American Academy in Rome, a Fellow of the Bogliasco Foundation, a recipient of two Asian Cultural Council residencies in Japan and a Master Artist of the Atlantic Center for the Arts. She is Danforth Professor of Dance at Mills College in residence during the spring semesters. For the remaining months of the year, she resides in New York City with her husband Roy Fowler.

Richard Move is artistic director of *MoveOpolis!*; a TEDGlobal Oxford Fellow; a PhD candidate in performance studies at New York University; assistant professor of dance in the Department of Drama, Theatre and Dance at Queens College, City University of New York; and lecturer in design at the Yale School of Drama. His commissions include productions for Mikhail Baryshnikov's White Oak Dance Project, Martha Graham Dance Company, PARADIGM, Opera Ballet of Florence, Helene Alexopoulos, Guggenheim Museum, American Festival of Paris, European Cultural Capitol, Parrish Art Museum, Deborah Harry and Blondie, Dame Shirley Bassey and Isaac Mizrahi. *MoveOpolis!* has been presented by New York Live Arts, the Kitchen, Jacob's Pillow, SiteLines/River-to-River Festival and on tour internationally. His films include *Bardo*, Jury Prize nominee at Lincoln Center's Dance on Camera Festival; *BloodWork: The Ana Mendieta Story*, National Board of Review Award / Directors Guild of America; *GhostLight*, Tribeca Film Festival premiere; and *GIMP: The Documentary*, 2014 Lincoln Center Dance on Camera Festival premiere. *Martha@ . . .*, Move's performances as Martha Graham, received two New York Dance and Performance Awards ('Bessies') and tours globally.

Bob Holman, a poet most often connected with spoken word, poetry slams, hip hop and digital poetry, began collaborating with Fenley at the Atlantic Center for the Arts where, along with their co-collaborator, the artist James Siena, they were in residence in 2008. Holman's modus operandi is to attend rehearsals, write on the fly (a ticklish, trained, tap-dancing know-it-all of a fly), consult with his dance guru Edwin Denby—and he and his poem often end up as part of the performance. Holman is the founder of the Bowery Poetry Club. He has published 16 books, most recently *Sing This One Back to Me*. He began his current work with the poetry of endangered languages while tracing the lineage of performance poetry to its root in orality and the world's oral traditions—particularly those of West African griots—which resulted in the PBS documentary, *Language Matters*, directed and produced by David Grubin. When performing with Fenley, Holman says, 'The words themselves are dancing too.'

Tere O'Connor has created over 40 works for his company and toured throughout the US, Europe, South America and Canada. He has created numerous commissioned works for other dance companies, including the Lyon Opera Ballet, White Oak Dance Project and solo works for Mikhail Baryshnikov and Jean Butler. O'Connor received a 2013 Doris Duke Performing Artist Award; he is a 2009 United States Artist Rockefeller Fellow and a 1993 Guggenheim Fellow. His work is supported by the National Endowment for the Arts, New England Foundation for the Arts / National Dance Project, The MAP Fund among many others. In October 2014, he was inducted into the American Academy of Arts and Sciences. An articulate and provocative educator, O'Connor has taught at festivals and universities around the globe for 25 years. He is a professor of dance at the University of Illinois, Urbana-Champaign.

Paz Tanjuaquio is a choreographer, performer a co-founding director of Topaz Arts, Inc. She first danced for Molissa Fenley in 1997 in the solo *Sita* at the Joyce Theater and has since performed in group works including *Credo in Us*; *Ice, Dew, Food, Crew, Ape*; *Lava Field*; *Delta*; *331 Steps*; and in the reconstructions of *Hemispheres*; *On the Other Ocean*; *Escalay*; *Short Stories*; *Sky Garden*; *Water Courses* and *Kuro Shio*. Her own choreography has been presented in New York at LaMaMa Moves, 92ndStY Harkness Dance Festival, the Danspace Project, Performance Space 122, Judson Church, Dance Theater Workshop; nationally at San Diego Trolley Dances, Cornell University, Kaatsbaan Dance Center; and internationally in artist residencies in Japan, South Korea, Cambodia, Vietnam and the Philippines. She received her MFA in dance from New York University and her BA in visual arts from University of California, San Diego. Awards for her work include National Endowment for the Arts, American Dance Festival's International Screendance and Meet The Composer / Commissioning USA among others.

David Moodey has collaborated with Molissa Fenley for nearly 30 years, lighting almost every dance she has created since 1987. In 1988, he received a Bessie Award for his design of Fenley's *State of Darkness*. Moodey is also the principal designer for Robert Ashley's modern opera, the Joffrey Ballet School and The Center for Discovery (who care for our most fragile fellow beings). Recent designs include *Crash*, a new modern opera composed by Robert Ashley, performed at the Whitney Museum for the 2014 Biennial; *The Nutcracker*, for the Joffrey Ballet School at the Skirball Theater, New York, and three new works for the Joffrey School Concert Group. Over the years, Moodey has had the pleasure of working with many talented artists including Peter Boal, Big Dance Theater, Meredith Monk, Sin Cha Hong, David Neumann and sculptor Carol Hepper. He is a member of both USA 829, the scenic artist union, and Local One, the Broadway stagehands union. He received his masters' degree in theater design from New York University.

Elizabeth Streb, choreographer, was born in 1950 and has been testing the potential of the human body ever since. The pre-eminent 'Extreme Action Architect', Streb is 'a rascal', 'a genius' and dance's answer to punk rock. She founded her company in 1985 and became a MacArthur Foundation Fellow in 1997. In 2003, she founded the STREB Lab for Action Mechanics (SLAM) in Williamsburg, Brooklyn. She also wrote the book

STREB: How to Become an Extreme Action Hero. The STREB Company has performed in, around and on top of major landmarks, theatres and stadiums worldwide. Streb is the subject of the 2014 documentary *Born to Fly*.

Rande Brown is an American writer and translator and holds a degree in East Asian studies from Princeton University. She was formerly the executive director of the Tricycle Foundation, publisher of *Tricycle: The Buddhist Review*. She is also president of East West Communications, a company that facilitates cultural understanding between Japan and the United States. Brown is a well-known translator of Japanese spiritual and cultural texts. She co-authored the *New York Times* bestseller *Geisha: A Life with Mineko Iwasaki*. She serves on the board of the New York Zen Center for Contemplative Care, under whose auspices she has been a volunteer chaplain at Beth Israel Medical Center in New York City. She received her Master of Social Work degree from New York University and is a licenced psychotherapist with a specific focus on the intersection of Buddhism, spirituality and psychology.

Stephen Greco is executive editor of Classical TV (www.classicaltv.com), the Internet destination for opera, ballet, modern dance, jazz and theatre videos; and editor-at-large of *Trace*, the international magazine focusing on 'transcultural styles and ideas'. A former senior editor of *Interview* magazine, *Stagebill* and the New York weekly *7 Days*, Greco has served as intelligence director of the True advertising agency and is a regular consultant on brand strategy and market intelligence to JWT, Landor, Office LAB, Gatard et Associés and Practical Semiotics. Greco has contributed features on arts and entertainment, style and fashion, youth culture and new media to publications such as *Advocate*, *American Way*, *Art News*, *Casa Vogue*, *Dance Magazine*, *Elle*, *Empire*, *Harper's Bazaar*, the London *Observer*, *New York* magazine, *New Yorker*, *New York Times Online*, *Opera News* and *San Francisco Chronicle*.

IMAGE 34 *Eureka* (1982); Molissa Fenley in photo session in New York; costume by Yonson Pak. Photograph by Jack Mitchell © 1982.

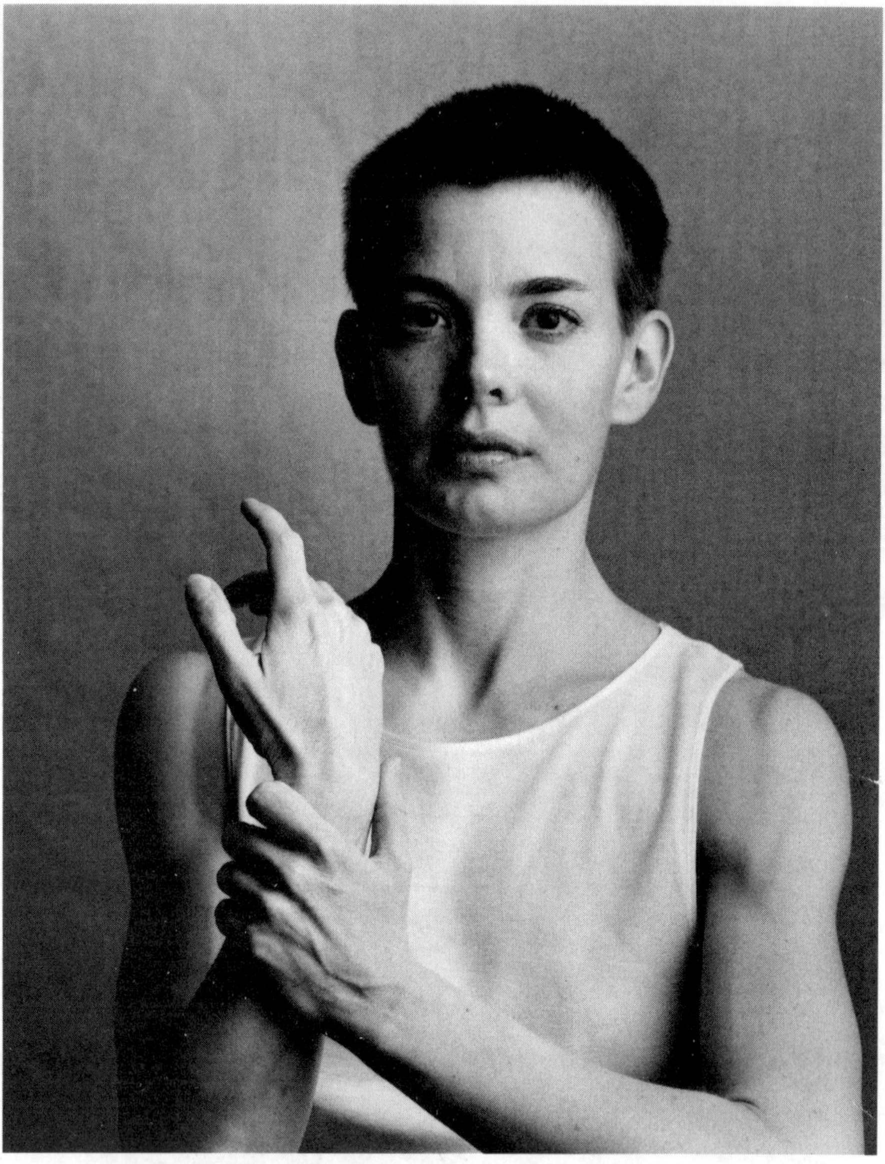

IMAGE 35 *Bardo* (1990); Molissa Fenley in photo session in New York. Photograph by Pierre Dufour © 1990.